Best Editorial Cartoons of the Year

LARTER · CALGARY SUN...

JOHN LARTER
Courtesy Calgary Sun

BEST EDITORIAL CARTOONS OF THE YEAR

1999 EDITION

Edited by
CHARLES BROOKS

PELICAN PUBLISHING COMPANY

Gretna 1999

Library of Congress Serial Catalog Data

Best editorial cartoons. 1972-
    Gretna [La.] Pelican Pub. Co.
    v. 29 cm annual-
"A pictorial history of the year."

    1. United States—Politics and government—
1969—Caricatures and Cartoons—Periodicals.
E839.5.B45   320.9'7309240207   73-643645
ISSN 0091-2220   MARC-S

Manufactured in the United States of America
Published by Pelican Publishing Company, Inc.
1000 Burmaster Street, Gretna, Louisiana 70053

Contents

Award-Winning Cartoons

1998 PULITZER PRIZE

SPEAKING OF CHARISMATIC CULT LEADERS and MASS SUICIDE...

STEVE BREEN

Editorial Cartoonist
Asbury Park Press

Born in Los Angeles, 1970; graduate of University of California, Riverside, in political science; won Scripps Howard's Charles M. Schulz Award as top college cartoonist, 1991; won John Locher Award for Outstanding College Editorial Cartoonist, 1991; artist, *Asbury Park Press,* New Jersey, 1994-1996; editorial cartoonist, *Asbury Park Press,* 1996 to the present.

1997 NATIONAL SOCIETY OF PROFESSIONAL JOURNALISTS AWARD
(Selected in 1998)

MICHAEL RAMIREZ

Editorial Cartoonist
Los Angeles Times

Born in Tokyo, Japan, 1961; graduated from the University of California at Irvine, 1984; editorial cartoonist for Baker Communications/Palos Verdes *Penninsula News,* 1983-90, the San Clemente *Daily Sun* and *Post,* 1989-90, the Memphis *Commercial Appeal,* 1989-90, and the Los Angeles *Times,* 1997 to the present; cartoons syndicated by Copley News Service; winner of the Pulitzer Prize for cartooning, 1994, and the Sigma Delta Chi Society of Professional Journalists Award for cartooning, 1995 and 1997; and president of the Association of American Editorial Cartoonists.

1998 JOHN FISCHETTI AWARD

JACK HIGGINS

Editorial Cartoonist
Chicago Sun-Times

Earned degree in economics, College of the Holy Cross; editorial cartoonist for the *Chicago Sun-Times,* 1984 to the present; winner of International Salon of Cartoons, 1988; Sigma Delta Chi National Society of Professional Journalists Award, 1988; Pulitzer Prize, 1989; and six Peter Lisagor Awards for editorial cartooning.

SERGE CHAPLEAU

Editorial Cartoonist
La Presse (Montreal)

Born in Montreal, Canada, 1945; caricaturist for various newspapers in
Montreal since 1971; editorial cartoonist for *La Presse* of Montreal.

Best Editorial Cartoons of the Year

MICHAEL RAMIREZ
Courtesy Los Angeles Times

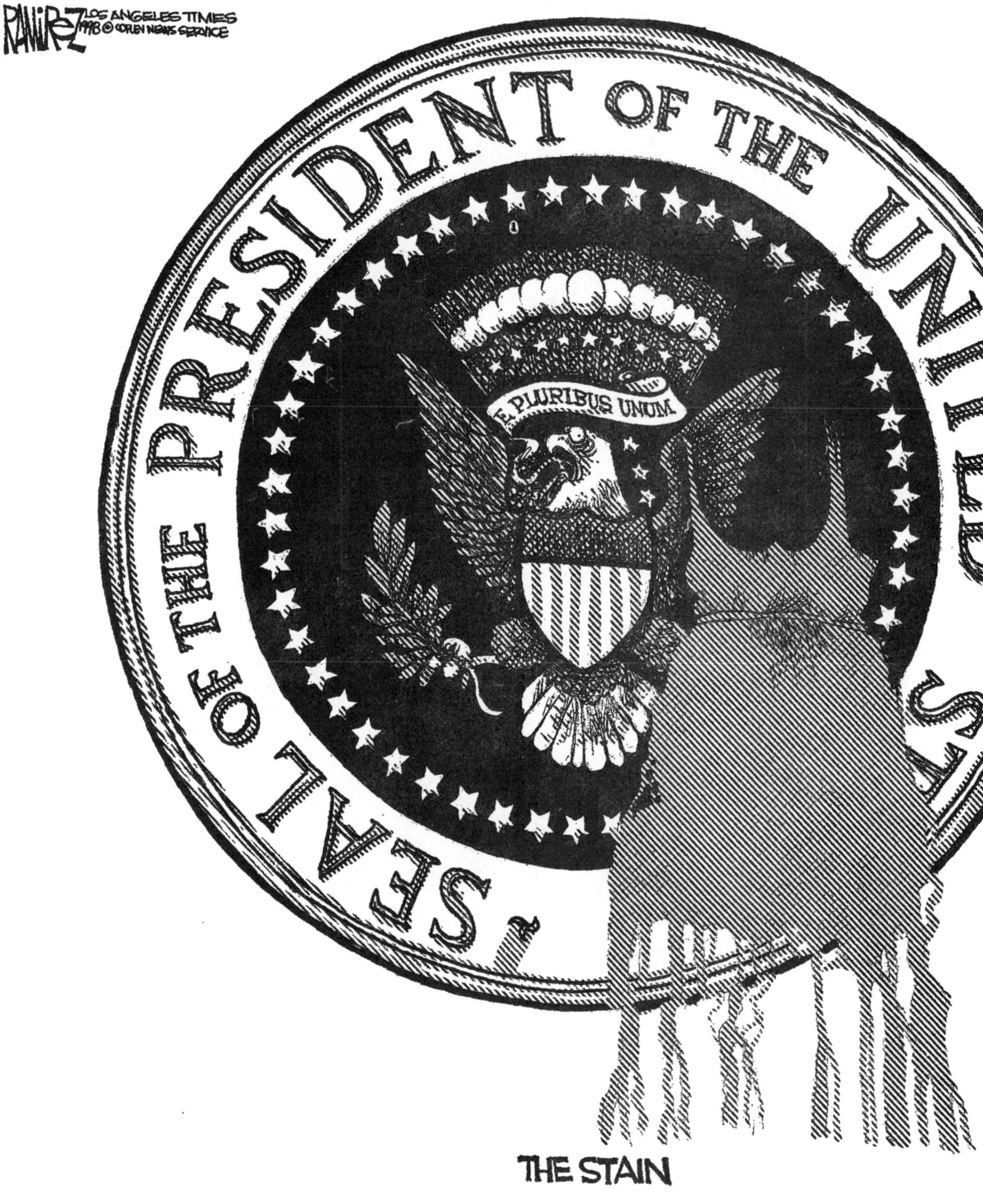
RAMIREZ LOS ANGELES TIMES 1998 © COPLEY NEWS SERVICE
SEAL OF THE PRESIDENT OF THE UNITED STATES
E PLURIBUS UNUM
THE STAIN

The Clinton Administration

The sex scandal linking President Clinton and former White House intern Monica Lewinsky broke in January and seldom left page one the rest of the year. Republican Kenneth Starr was appointed as independent counsel to investigate the charges made by Linda Tripp, a friend of Lewinsky. Eventually, Lewinsky was granted immunity in return for her testimony, and Clinton was subpoened to testify. It was a first for a sitting president.

After Starr's long-awaited report was released in September, Clinton finally settled a sexual harassment suit brought by Paula Jones by paying her $850,000. In December, the House of Representatives voted two articles of impeachment against the president. Clinton was accused of lying under oath and obstructing justice. It was only the second time in U.S. history that a president had been impeached. At year's end, the matter moved on to the Senate for trial.

On the eve of the House impeachment debate, Clinton ordered air strikes against Iraq. Saddam Hussein had repeatedly refused to allow United Nations inspectors access to suspected weapons sites. Some critics of the president saw political motives in the attack.

Republicans called for an investigation into reports that the Clinton administration had allowed sensitive missile technology to be given to China. Some charged that the transfer was payment for Chinese government donations to Clinton's presidential campaign. Attorney General Janet Reno, however, refused to act on the matter.

JOHN DEERING
Courtesy Arkansas Democrat

JOHN TREVER
Courtesy Albuquerque Journal

BOB LANG
Courtesy The News-Sentinel (Ind.)

MIKE RITTER
Courtesy Tribune Newspapers

DICK LOCHER
Courtesy Chicago Tribune

ACTUALLY, IT WAS ALL A VERBAL MISUNDERSTANDING...

WHAT I SAID WAS I NEVER HAD SAX WITH THAT WOMAN

DRAPER HILL
Courtesy Detroit News

I TRULY REGRET GETTING CAUGHT.

DARYL CAGLE
Courtesy Midweek (Hawaii)

MIKE KEEFE
Courtesy Denver Post

SORRY.

PRESIDENT OF

Mike Keefe THE DENVER POST.

16

LARRY WRIGHT
Courtesy Detroit News

JERRY BARNETT
Courtesy Indianapolis News

BOB ENGLEHART
Courtesy Hartford Courant

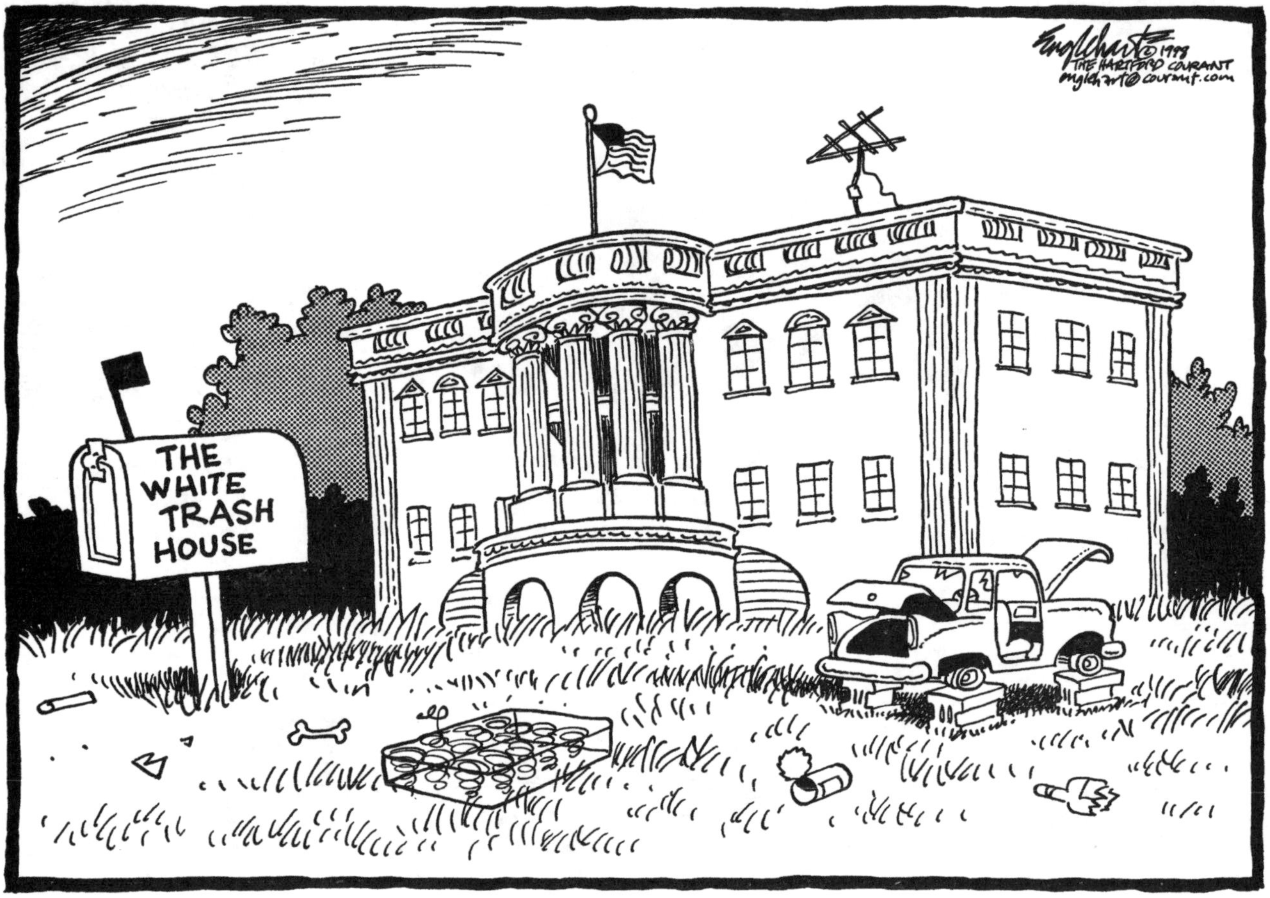
Englehart © 1998 THE HARTFORD COURANT englehart@courant.com
THE WHITE TRASH HOUSE

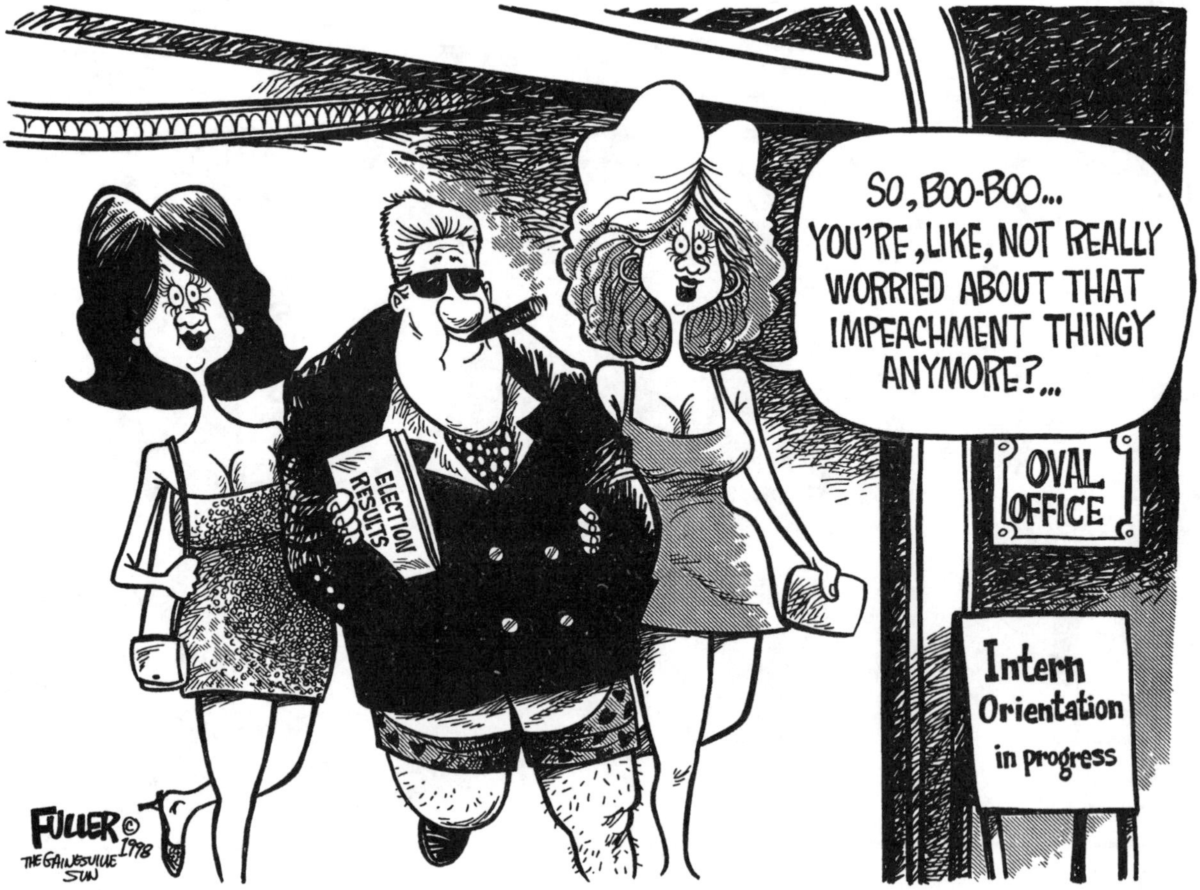
SO, BOO-BOO... YOU'RE, LIKE, NOT REALLY WORRIED ABOUT THAT IMPEACHMENT THINGY ANYMORE?...
ELECTION RESULTS
OVAL OFFICE
Intern Orientation in progress
FULLER © 1998 THE GAINESVILLE SUN

JAKE FULLER
Courtesy Gainesville Sun

BOB GORRELL
Courtesy Creators Syndicate

JIM BORGMAN
Courtesy Cincinnati Enquirer

JERRY BARNETT
Courtesy Indianapolis News

HANK MCCLURE
Courtesy Lawton Constitution (Okla.)

JIM BORGMAN
Courtesy Cincinnati Enquirer

BILL GARNER
Courtesy Washington Times

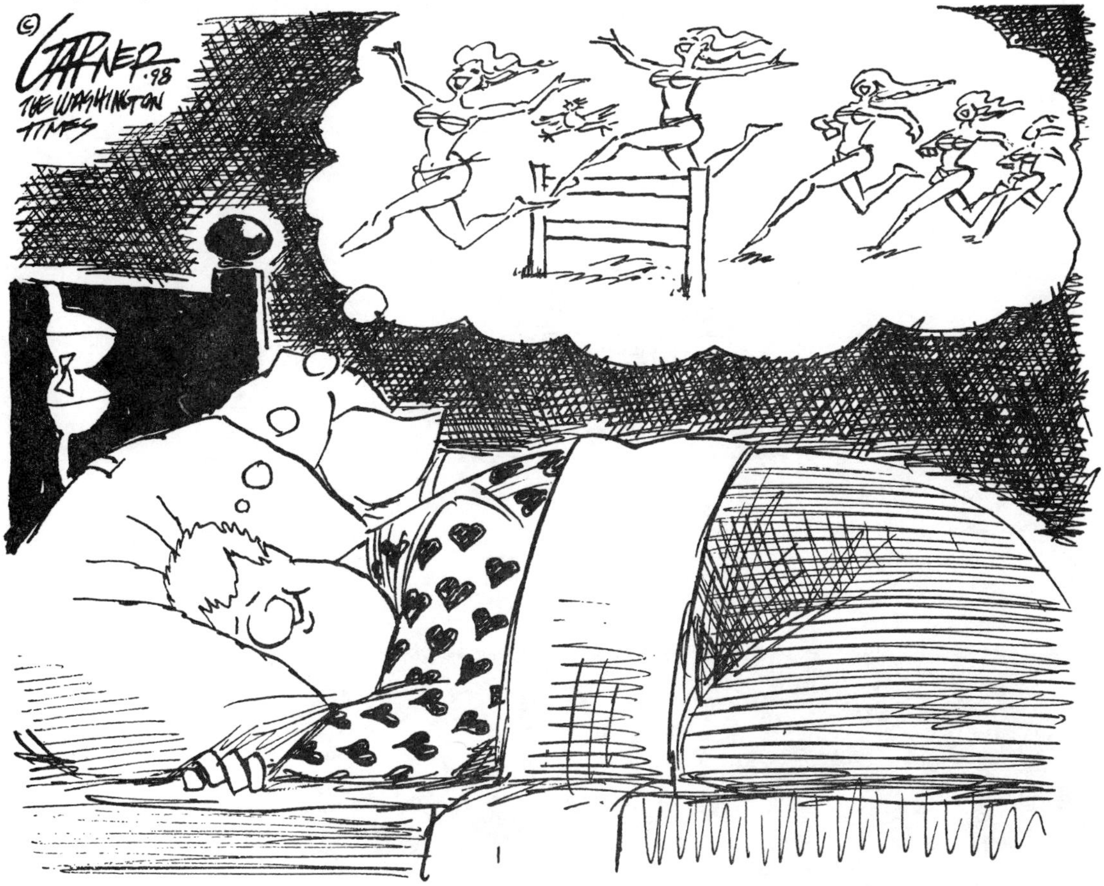

© GARNER '98 THE WASHINGTON TIMES

JERRY HOLBERT
Courtesy Boston Herald

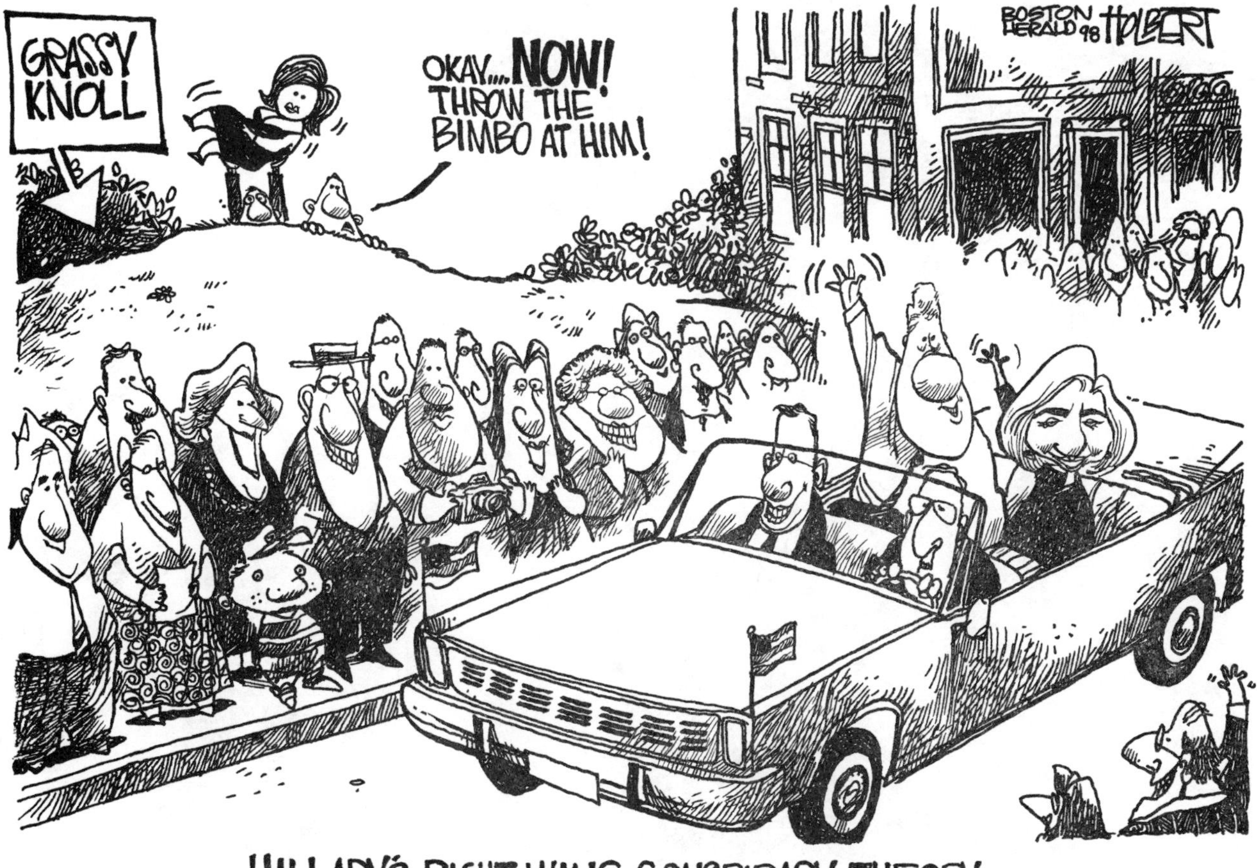

BOSTON HERALD '98 HOLBERT
GRASSY KNOLL
OKAY... NOW! THROW THE BIMBO AT HIM!
HILLARY'S RIGHT-WING CONSPIRACY THEORY

BILL GARNER
Courtesy Washington Times

MIKE PETERS
Courtesy Dayton Daily News

SIGNE WILKINSON
Courtesy Philadelphia Daily News

TED RALL
Courtesy San Francisco Examiner

JOE HELLER
Courtesy Green Bay Press-Gazette

"FIND OUT WHO HER PLASTIC SURGEON IS..."

WAYNE STAYSKAL
Courtesy Tampa Tribune

KEVIN KALLAUGHER
Courtesy Baltimore Sun

JACK HIGGINS
Courtesy Chicago Sun-Times

GLENN MCCOY
Courtesy Belleville News-Democrat

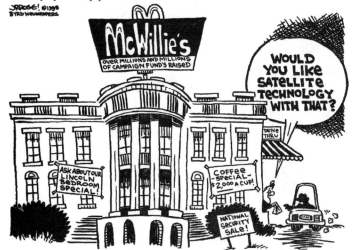

J. R. ROSE
Courtesy Byrd Newspapers

JIM LANGE
Courtesy Daily Oklahoman

SCOTT STANTIS
Courtesy Birmingham News

DICK LOCHER
Courtesy Chicago Tribune

ED GAMBLE
Courtesy Florida Times-Union

SERGE CHAPLEAU
Courtesy La Presse (Montreal)

ED GAMBLE
Courtesy Florida Times-Union

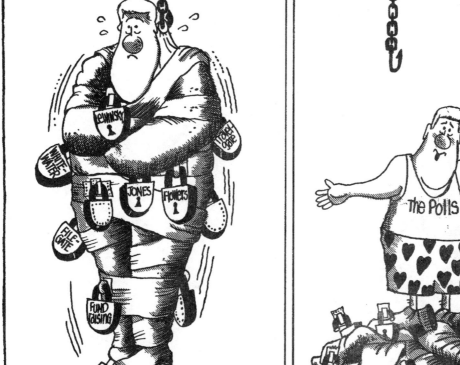

28

CHIP BECK
Courtesy The Real Washington (D.C.)

KEVIN KALLAUGHER
Courtesy Baltimore Sun

CHIP BOK
Courtesy Akron Beacon Journal

29

JEFF MACNELLY
Courtesy Chicago Tribune

ROBERT ARIAIL
Courtesy The State (S.C.)

WILLIAM L. FLINT
Courtesy Arlington Morning News

RICKY NOBILE
Courtesy Mississippi Business Journal

S. C. RAWLS
Courtesy NEA

SERGE CHAPLEAU
Courtesy La Presse (Montreal)

ED STEIN
Courtesy Rocky Mountain News

WAYNE STAYSKAL
Courtesy Tampa Tribune

MIKE LANE
Courtesy Baltimore Sun

KIRK ANDERSON
Courtesy St. Paul Pioneer Press

SIGNE WILKINSON
Courtesy Philadelphia Daily News

SIZE DOES MATTER

KIRK WALTERS
Courtesy Toledo Blade

MARK THORNHILL
Courtesy North County Times

35

JIM BERRY
Courtesy NEA

Berry's World

NUCLEAR PROLIFERATION HUMAN RIGHTS ABORTION DALAI LAMA ETC.

← CAMPAIGN CONTRIBUTIONS

You've got to take a little bad with the good.

I CALL IT, "PRESIDENTIAL DIGNITY".

LINDA BOILEAU
Courtesy Frankfort State Journal

JOHN BRANCH
Courtesy San Antonio Express-News

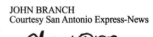

SEX!

Bill Clinton
My Place in History

SCANDAL!

MOVING DAY?

JIM MILLER
Courtesy Danville Valley Citizen (Calif.)

STEVE BREEN
Courtesy Asbury Park Press (N.J.)

DANA SUMMERS
Courtesy Orlando Sentinel

MIKE SMITH
Courtesy Las Vegas Sun

DARRYL BARKSDALE
Courtesy Santa Cruz County Sentinel

Kenneth Starr

In 1983, at the age of 37, Kenneth Starr was named to the U.S. Court of Appeals for the District of Columbia, the youngest person ever to receive the lifetime appointment. His judicial integrity inspired great respect, even among colleagues who disagreed with his views. Starr subsequently was named solicitor general under President George Bush, but returned to the private sector when Bill Clinton was elected.

Life for Starr was to change forever when a three-judge panel appointed him to serve as independent counsel for the criminal inquiry into alleged Clinton wrongdoing in the Whitewater land development deal. Starr reopened the investigation that had been begun by U.S. attorney Robert Fiske, and then expanded it as other serious allegations arose. Starr's office was responsible for convictions against former Arkansas governor Jim Guy Tucker, as well as former Clinton associates Jim and Susan McDougal.

In January 1988, Linda Tripp, a Pentagon employee, gave Starr secretly recorded tapes of conversations she had had with Monica Lewinsky. The tapes contained some 20 hours of conversations in which Lewinsky spoke at great length about having had an affair with President Clinton. The rest is history.

STEVE KELLEY
Courtesy San Diego Union

JAMES GRASDAL
Courtesy Edmonton Journal (Alberta)

VIC CANTONE
Courtesy Brooklyn Paper Publications

BRUMSIC BRANDON, JR.
Courtesy Florida Today

LAZARO FRESQUET
Courtesy El Nuevo Herald (Miami)

JON RICHARDS
Courtesy Santa Fe Reporter

YOUR TAX DOLLARS AT WORK

ED FISCHER
Courtesy Rochester Post-Bulletin

ED FISCHER
© 1998 Rochester Post-Bulletin Co. LLC.
Ed Fischer Syndicate
fischer@postbulletin.com
Clinton in the Polls
Starr
sex scandal

GEORGE DANBY
Courtesy Bangor Daily News

BANGORNEWS.com
DANBY
©1998 BANGOR DAILY NEWS
THE UNITED STATES MEANS BUSINESS... A SUBPOENA FROM KEN STARR!
SADDAM
IRAQ
FILE

NICK ANDERSON
Courtesy Louisville Courier-Journal

THE PUNISHMENT SHOULD FIT THE CRIME...
STARR

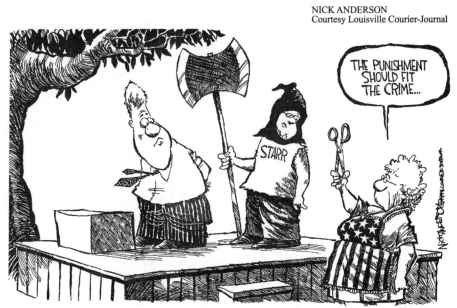

CHESTER COMMODORE
Courtesy Chicago Daily Defender

JEFF MACNELLY
Courtesy Chicago Tribune

ROB CHAMBERS
Courtesy The Signal (Calif.)

JAKE FULLER
Courtesy Gainesville Sun

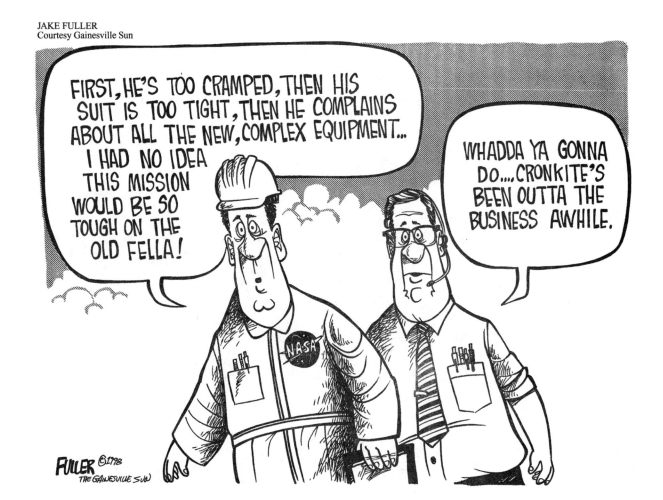

The Media

The reputation of the news media did not fare well in 1998. CNN committed a *faux pas* when it reported that the U.S. military had used nerve gas against American deserters in the Vietnam War. Both former and current military leaders angrily denied the charges, and the network withdrew the story and apologized.

A Cincinnati *Enquirer* reporter was fired for a series of stories alleging that banana giant Chiquita bribed foreign officials and used life-threatening pesticides on its fruit. An apology was issed in bold type. The *New Republic* disclosed that parts of 27 articles a reporter had written for the magazine had been fabricated. A week later, a prize-winning reporter for the Boston *Globe* was forced to resign for similar offenses.

Campaign advertisements hit a new low for mudslinging and name-calling prior to the November elections. Many people thought that television went too far late in the year when Dr. Jack Kevorkian (also known as Dr. Death) was shown in a live broadcast giving a man a lethal injection. After the show, Kevorkian was indicted for murder.

CLAY BENNETT
Courtesy Christian Science Monitor

Television

High-Definition Television

JOHN MARSHALL
Courtesy Binghamton Press
& Sun-Bulletin

MARK PETT
Courtesy Deseret News (Utah)

46

BOB DORNFRIED
Courtesy Fairfield Citizen News (Conn.)

SCOTT BATEMAN
Courtesy North American Syndicate

STEVE GREENBERG
Courtesy Seattle Post-Intelligencer

REX BABIN
Courtesy Albany Times Union (N.Y.)

NICK ANDERSON
Courtesy Louisville Courier-Journal

STEVE YORK
Courtesy Kankakee Daily Journal

Berry's World

© 1998 by NEA, Inc.

JIM BERRY
Courtesy NEA

Which 'Seinfeld' character *will* NBC miss the most?

A) Jerry

B) Elaine

C) Kramer

D) George

© 1998 Barbara Brandon/Dist. by Universal Press Syndicate

BARBARA BRANDON-CROFT
Courtesy Universal Press Syndicate

50

KEVIN KALLAUGHER
Courtesy Baltimore Sun

JERRY BARNETT
Courtesy Indianapolis News

JEFF MACNELLY
Courtesy Chicago Tribune

ROB ROGERS
Courtesy Pittsburgh Post-Gazette

Foreign Affairs

After Saddam Hussein repeatedly barred United Nations inspectors from suspected weapons sites, President Clinton ordered missile strikes against Iraq. The four-night barrage by the U.S. and Great Britain did not seem to faze the mercurial Iraqi leader.

Simultaneous bombings of U.S. embassies in Kenya and Tanzania claimed the lives of more than 100 victims, including 11 Americans. In retaliation, the U.S. fired cruise missiles at a terrorist camp in Afghanistan and a suspected weapons plant in Sudan. The timing of the bombardment, when Monica Lewinsky was testifying about her sexual relationship with President Clinton, suggested to many people a "Wag the Dog" scenario. The movie "Wag the Dog," filmed before the Clinton-Lewinsky affair was made public, shows an American president staging a war to distract public attention from allegations of sexual misconduct.

Russia's sagging economy and Boris Yeltsin's failing health continued to threaten world political stability. President Clinton traveled to Russia to wrestle with the problems. Japan and Indonesia faced severe economic problems throughout the year. Leaders from Israel, Jordan, and the PLO met with Clinton in search of a Middle East peace agreement, but lasting peace remained elusive. Pakistan and India angered the world by conducting nuclear tests, and Pope John Paul II made a historic visit to Cuba.

SCOTT STANTIS
Courtesy Birmingham News

53

DAVE GRANLUND
Courtesy Middlesex News

BILL GARNER
Courtesy Washington Times

JERRY HOLBERT
Courtesy Boston Herald

JEFF MACNELLY
Courtesy Chicago Tribune

JOHN LARTER
Courtesy Calgary Sun

ROY PETERSON
Courtesy Vancouver Sun

SIZE DOES MATTER.

MARK THORNHILL
Courtesy North County Times

DREW SHENEMAN
Courtesy Newark Star-Ledger

KIRK WALTERS
Courtesy Toledo Blade

FRED CURATOLO
Courtesy Edmonton Sun (Alberta)

ANN TELNAES
Courtesy North American Syndicate

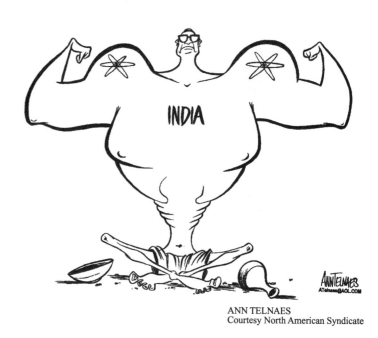

CLAY JONES
Courtesy Free Lance-Star (Va.)

JOHN TREVER
Courtesy Albuquerque Journal

RIVERDANCE

CHAN LOWE
Courtesy Fort Lauderdale News /
Sun Sentinel

"WHY, NO... WE HAVE NO CATHOLIC OR PROTESTANT DISTRICTS HERE."

JIM BERRY
Courtesy NEA

FRED CURATOLO
Courtesy Edmonton Sun (Alberta)

JOHN DEERING
Courtesy Arkansas Democrat

STUART CARLSON
Courtesy Milwaukee Journal Sentinel

GARY MCCOY
Courtesy Suburban Journals (Ill.)

JAMES MCCLOSKEY
Courtesy Staunton Daily News Leader

saving
private yeltsin

JAMES MERCADO
Courtesy Honolulu Advertiser

CHIP BOK
Courtesy Akron Beacon Journal

WALT HANDELSMAN
Courtesy New Orleans Times-Picayune

NICK ANDERSON
Courtesy Louisville Courier-Journal

ROBERT ARIAIL
Courtesy The State (S.C.)

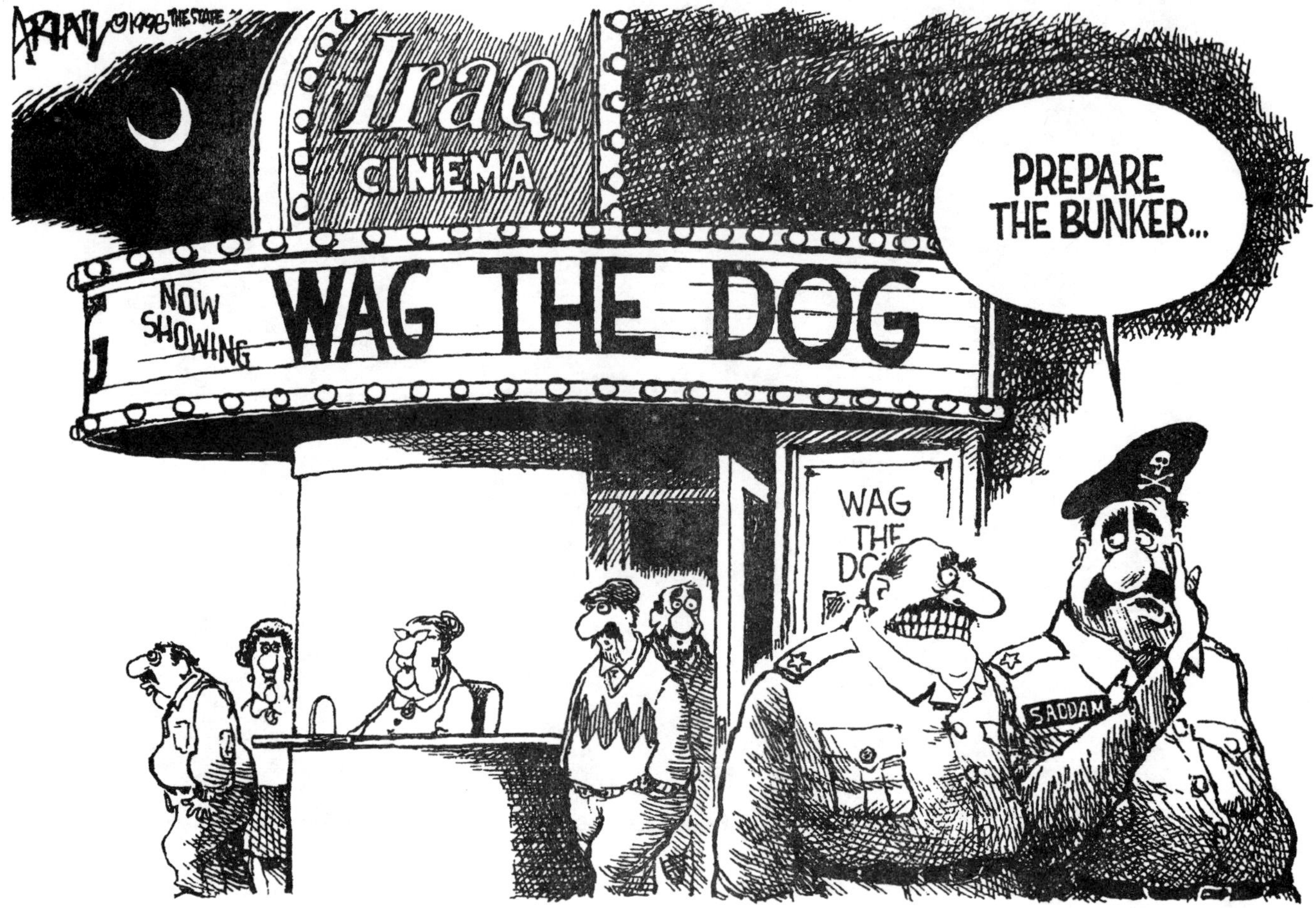
ARIAIL ©1998 THE STATE
Iraq
CINEMA
NOW SHOWING
WAG THE DOG
PREPARE THE BUNKER...
SADDAM

RICK MCKEE
Courtesy Augusta Chronicle

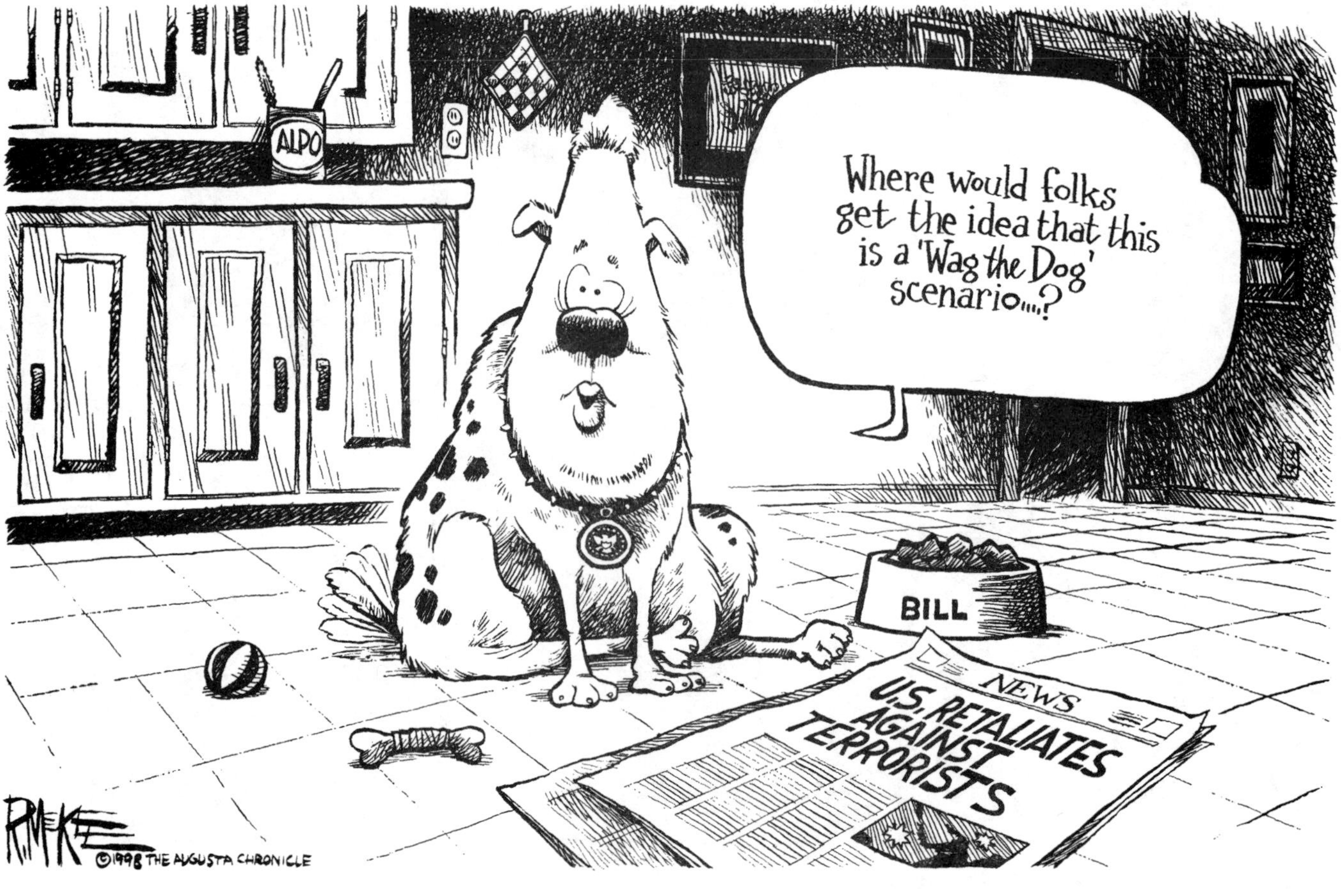
ALPO
Where would folks get the idea that this is a 'Wag the Dog' scenario.....?
BILL
NEWS
U.S. RETALIATES AGAINST TERRORISTS
R. MCKEE ©1998 THE AUGUSTA CHRONICLE

ED STEIN
Courtesy Rocky Mountain News

MIKE KEEFE
Courtesy Denver Post

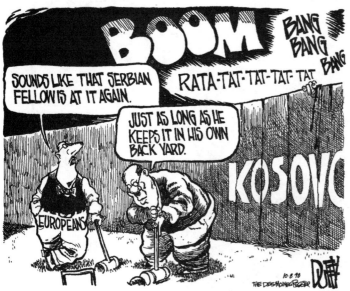

BRIAN DUFFY
Courtesy Des Moines Register

ROY PETERSON
Courtesy Vancouver Sun

JAMES CASCIARI
Courtesy Vero Beach Press Journal

SCOTT STANTIS
Courtesy Birmingham News

J. R. ROSE
Courtesy Byrd Newspapers

BOB GORRELL
Courtesy Creators Syndicate

KIRK ANDERSON
Courtesy St. Paul Pioneer Press

MIKE PETERS
Courtesy Dayton Daily News

JEFF DANZIGER
Courtesy Los Angeles Times Syndicate

DALE STEPHANOS
Courtesy Boston Herald

MIKE PETERS
Courtesy Dayton Daily News

DICK LOCHER
Courtesy Chicago Tribune

MIKE LUCKOVICH
Courtesy Atlanta Constitution

A game of cat and mouse

JEFF DANZIGER
Courtesy Los Angeles Times Syndicate

ED GAMBLE
Courtesy Florida Times-Union

JIM BORGMAN
Courtesy Cincinnati Enquirer

SIGNE WILKINSON
Courtesy Philadelphia Daily News

FRANK CAMMUSO
Courtesy Syracuse Herald-Journal

JOHN SHERFFIUS
Courtesy St. Louis Post-Dispatch

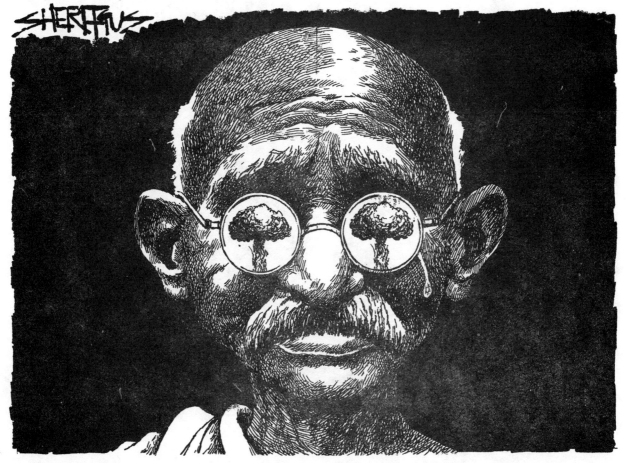

DAVID HITCH
Courtesy Worcester Telegram &
Gazette (Mass.)

JIM LANGE
Courtesy Daily Oklahoman

JACK HIGGINS
Courtesy Chicago Sun-Times

STEVE MCBRIDE
Courtesy Independence Daily Reporter

The Nuclear Community awakens to a new Monster.

DOUG MACGREGOR
Courtesy News-Press at Fort Myers

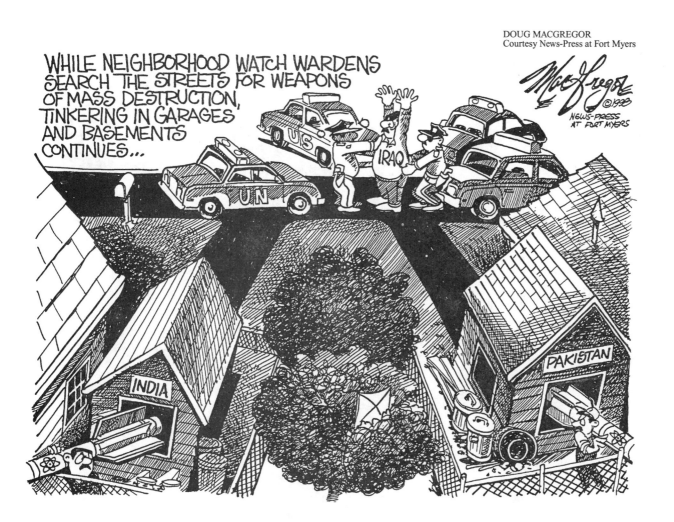

75

SCOTT STANTIS
Courtesy Birmingham News

GERALD AVERA
Courtesy The Tribune & Georgian

The Republicans

House Speaker Newt Gingrich was calling the shots for Republicans for much of the year. The GOP was nervous about possible impeachment hearings and for a time all but ruled them out until 1999. Then Independent Counsel Ken Starr was invited to come to the Hill to present evidence he had assembled on the Clinton-Lewinsky affair. He did so, and it proved to be more than the public wanted to hear.

The Republicans dropped steadily in the polls while Democratic prospects soared. Most pundits, even Democratic sympathizers, still felt that the GOP would gain seats in the November elections. Instead, the Democrats made unexpected gains, reducing the Republican majority in the House to a handful of seats. Gingrich, a former history professor, saw the writing on the wall and resigned the speakership.

For much of the year, Republicans had not pushed their conservative agenda. Polls showed that voters felt the majority party was trying to move too far too fast. Surveys suggested that tax cuts, for example, were not generally favored by the voters. President Clinton always seemed to read the mood of the voters better. While the Republicans had hoped to offer a choice between Democratic spending and their own tax cuts, support for increased spending had grown within the GOP ranks. Furthermore, the balanced budget made it more difficult to oppose Clinton's expensive spending programs. At year's end, the Republican Party seemed to be in disarray, uncertain about what course to take next.

MIKE LUCKOVICH
Courtesy Atlanta Constitution

MIKE LANE
Courtesy Baltimore Sun

ANN TELNAES
Courtesy North American Syndicate

ED GAMBLE
Courtesy Florida Times-Union

DAVE GRANLUND
Courtesy Metrowest Daily News

BRIAN DUFFY
Courtesy Des Moines Register

MIKE LANE
Courtesy Baltimore Sun

JERRY BUCKLEY
Courtesy Express Newspapers

ROBERT ARIAIL
Courtesy The State (S.C.)

JEFF KOTERBA
Courtesy Omaha World-Herald

MATT DAVIES
Courtesy Gannett Suburban Newspapers

SCOTT STANTIS
Courtesy Birmingham News

MIKE PETERS
Courtesy Dayton Daily News

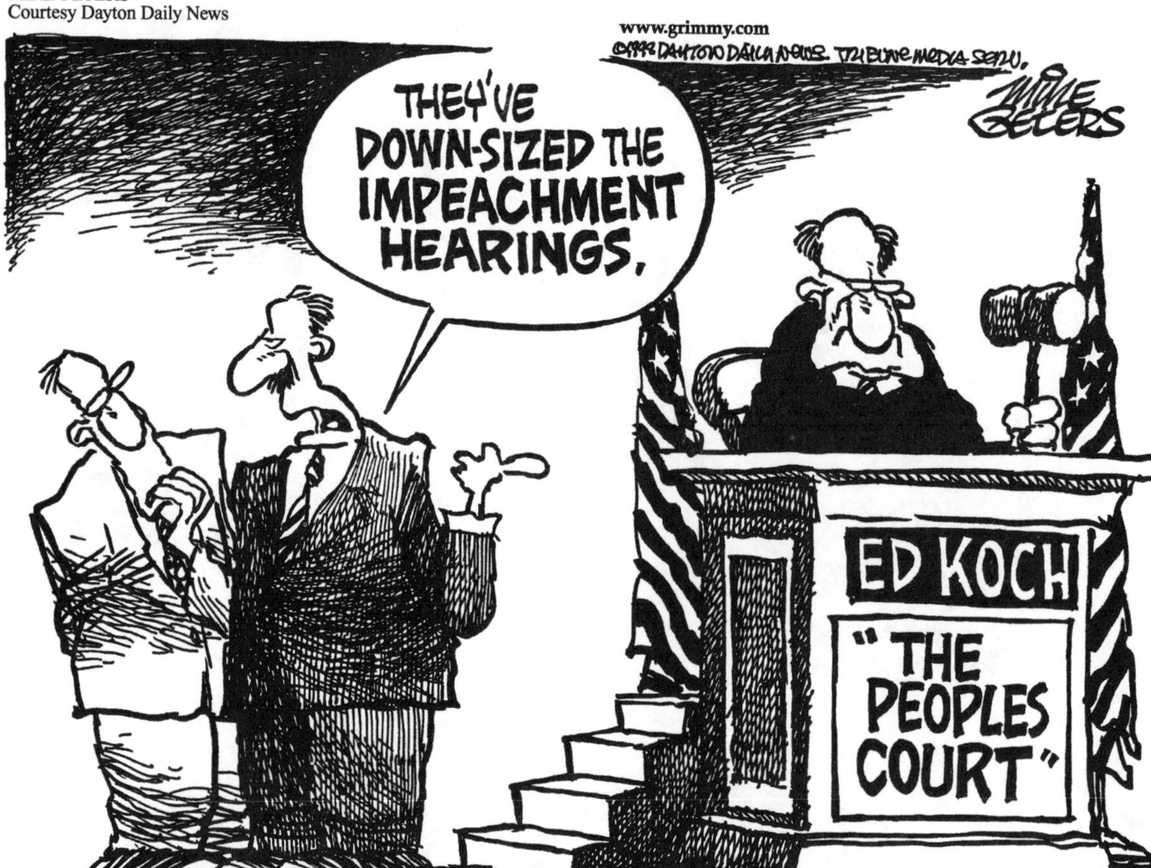

www.grimmy.com
THEY'VE DOWN-SIZED THE IMPEACHMENT HEARINGS.
ED KOCH
"THE PEOPLES COURT"

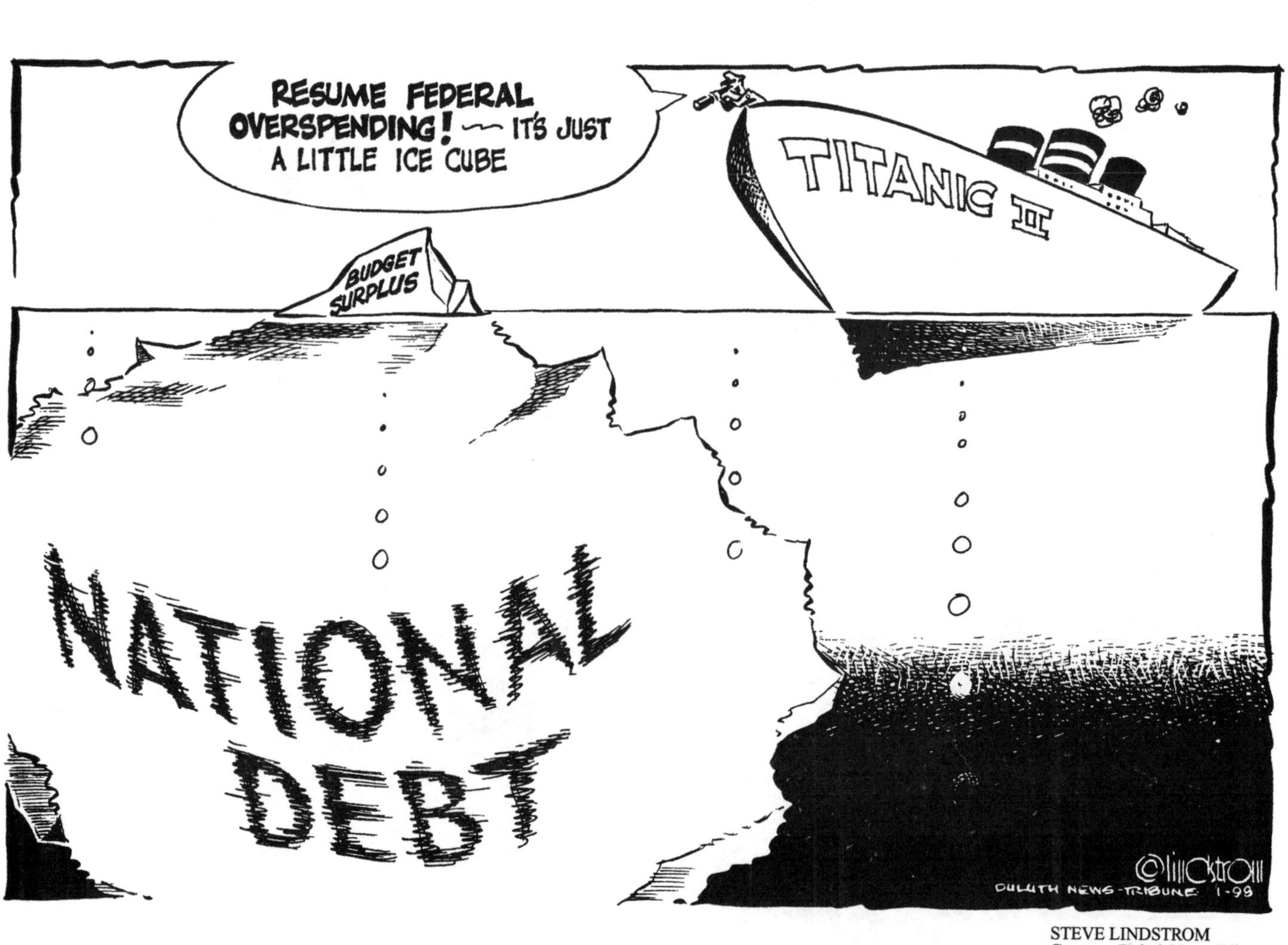

RESUME FEDERAL OVERSPENDING! — IT'S JUST A LITTLE ICE CUBE
TITANIC II
BUDGET SURPLUS
NATIONAL DEBT
DULUTH NEWS-TRIBUNE 1-98

STEVE LINDSTROM
Courtesy Duluth News-Tribune

Congress

Early in the year, the Treasury Department disclosed that for the first time since 1970 the government took in more money in taxes than it spent in 1997. Surpluses of $100 to $200 billion are expected during the next five years. On hearing the news, Congress wasted no time in scrambling to decide what to do with the windfall. Some wanted to cut taxes, while others began lining up pork barrel projects.

Republican Sen. Fred Thompson headed a committee to look into campaign finance reform. But the initiative folded when it became apparent that neither the public nor the media was interested. For 200 years, the tobacco industry seemed to have Congress in its pocket, but in 1998 that changed. By the year's end, Congress had passed laws prohibiting billboards that urged a relaxing puff, brand-pegged merchandise, and cartoon ads to attract teenagers. The tobacco companies agreed to pay $206 billion in damages to 46 states.

Democrats scored impressive gains in mid-term elections, and House Speaker Newt Gingrich was forced to give up his post. He also announced he would leave Congress. The many changes Congress passed in an effort to reform welfare seemed to be working. More and more people were trimmed from welfare rolls, and state agencies were helping find jobs and giving assistance where it appeared to be needed.

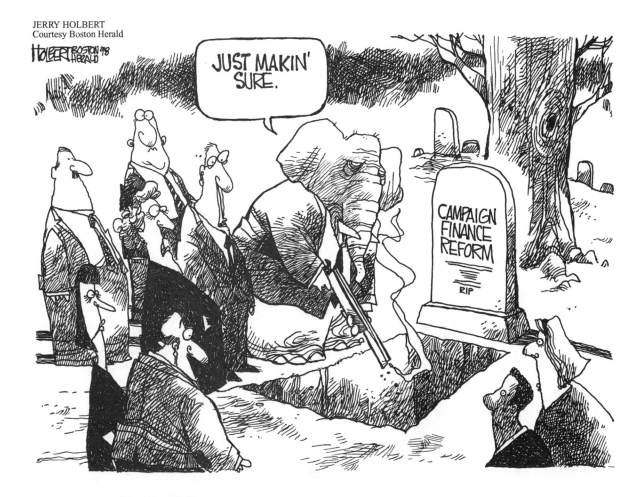

JERRY HOLBERT
Courtesy Boston Herald

CHIP BOK
Courtesy Akron Beacon Journal

BOB DORNFRIED
Courtesy Fairfield Citizen News (Conn.)

ETTA HULME
Courtesy Fort Worth Star-Telegram

BOB LANG
Courtesy The News-Sentinel (Ind.)

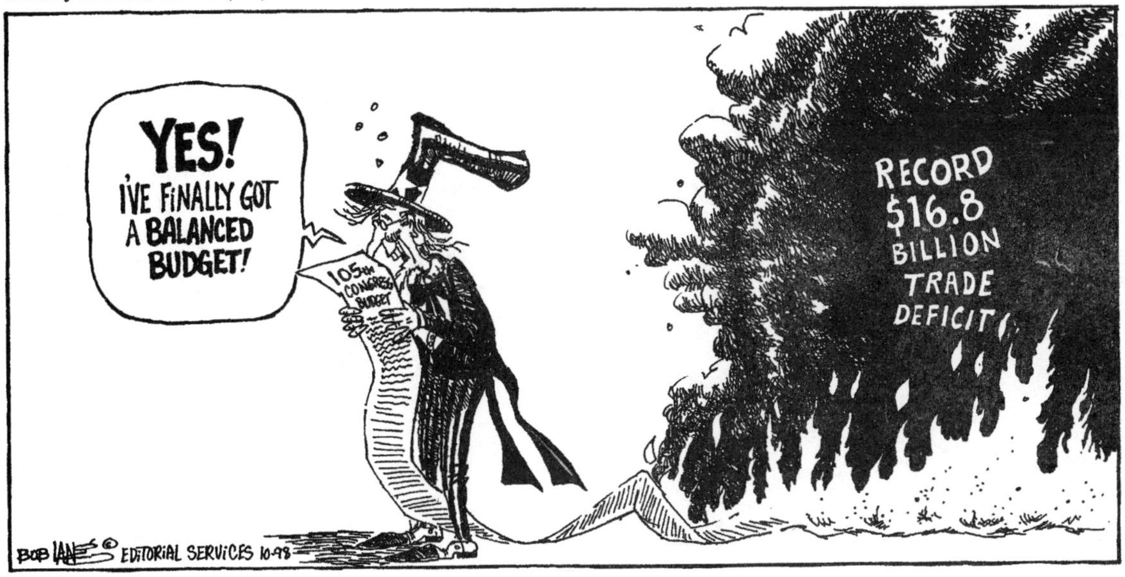
YES! I'VE FINALLY GOT A BALANCED BUDGET!
105th CONGRESS BUDGET
RECORD $16.8 BILLION TRADE DEFICIT
BOB LANG © EDITORIAL SERVICES 10-98

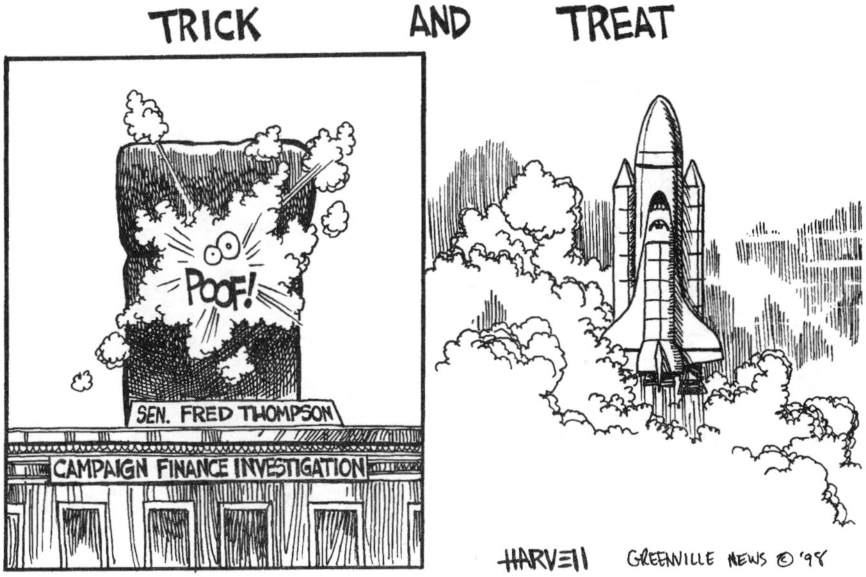
TRICK AND TREAT
POOF!
SEN. FRED THOMPSON
CAMPAIGN FINANCE INVESTIGATION
HARVELL GREENVILLE NEWS © '98

ROGER HARVELL
Courtesy Greenville News (S.C.)

ETTA HULME
Courtesy Fort Worth Star-Telegram

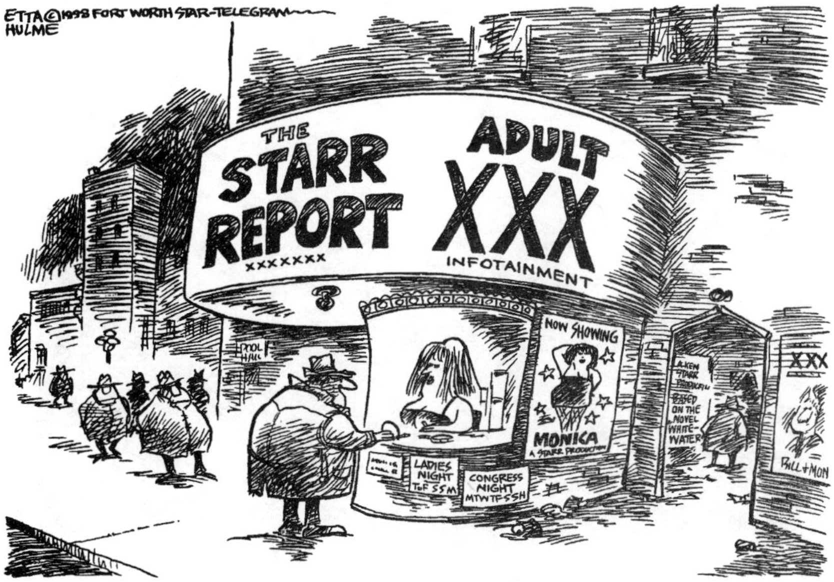
ETTA HULME ©1998 FORT WORTH STAR-TELEGRAM
THE STARR REPORT
XXXXXXX
ADULT XXX
INFOTAINMENT
NOW SHOWING
MONICA
A STARR PRODUCTION
LADIES NIGHT TUE SS M
CONGRESS NIGHT MTWTFSSH
POOL HALL
A KEN STARR PRODUCTION
BASED ON THE NOVEL WHITE-WATER
XXX
BILL+MON

ED FISCHER
Courtesy Rochester Post-Bulletin

CHUCK ASAY
Courtesy Colorado Springs Gazette

KIRK ANDERSON
Courtesy St. Paul Pioneer Press

Politics

Attorney General Janet Reno was pressured throughout the year to call an investigation into reports that the Clinton administration had allowed sensitive missile technology to be sent to China. Some critics charged that the technology transfer was payment for Chinese donations to the Clinton campaign in 1992. Reno declined to pursue the matter.

A budget surplus was announced during the year, and arguments immediately began over how to spend it. Some wanted to use it to strengthen Social Security, others wanted tax cuts, and still others wanted to take care of various special interest groups around the country. The president's job approval ratings remained high while the reading on Congress was mixed at best.

Because of the unexpectedly poor showing by the Republicans in congressional races, House Speaker Newt Gingrich immediately resigned his position. The Democrats gained 5 seats in the House, a stunning achievement in historical terms, and held its 45 seats in the Senate. A major surprise came in Minnesota, where former professional wrestler Jesse Ventura, an independent, defeated Republican and Democratic candidates for governor.

Feminist groups continued to maintain a deafening silence in the Clinton-Lewinsky matter, confirming once again that their commitment to politics outweighs their commitment to women.

ED TAYLOR
Courtesy The Daily Iowan

87

CHARLIE DANIEL
Courtesy Knoxville News-Sentinel

TIM HARTMAN
Courtesy North Hills News Record (Pa.)

LOU GRANT
Courtesy The Montclarion (Calif.)

TOM BECK
Courtesy Freeport Journal-Standard (Ill.)

Berry's World

WHAT DO THE POLLS SAY THAT I SHOULD DO AND SAY NEXT?

ACCORDING TO THE POLLS, WHAT SHOULD I DO AND SAY NEXT?

© 1998 by NEA, Inc.

JIM BERRY
Courtesy NEA

JAMES MCCLOSKEY
Courtesy Staunton Daily News Leader

NONSENSE... THEY'RE GLASSES!

JIMMY MARGULIES
Courtesy Hackensack Record

The GRAMMYS

MARGULIES
©1998 THE RECORD
www.bergen.com/margulies

Ken Starr presents Best Recording Artist award to Linda Tripp

MATT DAVIES
Courtesy Gannett Suburban Newspapers

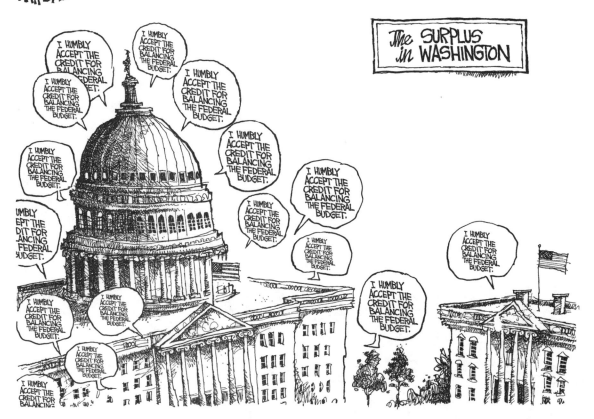

PAUL DUGINSKI
Courtesy Los Angeles Times

MILT PRIGGEE
Courtesy Spokane Spokesman-Review

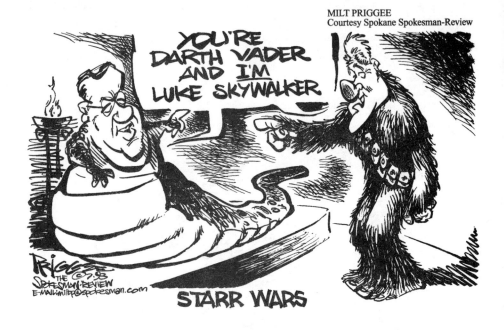

CLAY BENNETT
Courtesy Christian Science Monitor

The Great American Political Debate

GARY VARVEL
Courtesy Indianapolis Star

Berry's World

PICK OUT THE BAD GUY
ONE MAN LIED UNDER OATH. THE OTHER MAN IS A SPECIAL PROSECUTOR.

© 1998 by NEA, Inc.

Jim Berry

HINT: BAD GUYS WEAR BLACK HATS.

STEVE MCBRIDE
Courtesy Independence Daily Reporter

PAUL CONRAD
Courtesy Los Angeles Times Syndicate

STEPHEN TEMPLETON
Courtesy Charlottesville Daily

BILL GARNER
Courtesy Washington Times

TOM GIBB
Courtesy Johnstown Tribune-
Democrat

THE GROWTH CHART

WALT HANDELSMAN
Courtesy New Orleans Times-Picayune

CHARLIE DANIEL
Courtesy Knoxville News-Sentinel

WAYNE STAYSKAL
Courtesy Tampa Tribune

MIKE SMITH
Courtesy Las Vegas Sun

JACK HIGGINS
Courtesy Chicago Sun-Times

STEVE KELLEY
Courtesy San Diego Union
©1998 SAN DIEGO UNION TRIBUNE
COPLEY NEWS SERVICE

WAYNE STAYSKAL
Courtesy Tampa Tribune

JOHN TREVER
Courtesy Albuquerque Journal

ERIC SMITH
Courtesy Annapolis Capital Gazette

STEVE BREEN
Courtesy Asbury Park Press (N.J.)

The Economy

As 1998 dawned, the dire economic situation throughout Asia threatened to drag down the U.S. economy with it. The Asian crisis spilled over into Russia, Latin America, Japan, and much of the rest of the world. Banks clamped down on lending, and the Federal Reserve cut interest rates three times. The stock market went on a wild rollercoaster ride. It peaked in July, fell back in the fall, but recovered by the end of the year.

Bill Gates and Microsoft battled the federal government over accusations that the software giant was engaged in unfair business practices that, in fact, made it a monopoly. Gates argued that his rivals employ the same tactics that he does. In any event, Microsoft is giving customers a good product at a cheaper price, and competitors continue to howl.

The year 2000 (or Y2K) looms as a crisis of worldwide proportions in the minds of some observers. They believe that when the new year dawns, computers will be fooled into thinking that the year 1900 has arrived because programs were written with only two digits for dates. Dire predictions have been made. No one is sure just what damage the millenium bug will cause. It conceivably could play havoc, and governments and businesses were at work on the potential problem as the year ended.

MIKE THOMPSON
Courtesy Copley News Service

ED FISCHER
Courtesy Rochester Post-Bulletin

JOE HOFFECKER
Courtesy Cincinnati Business Journal

PAM WINTERS
Courtesy San Diego Union Tribune
& North County Times

S. C. RAWLS
Courtesy NEA

JOHN KOVALIC
Courtesy Wisconsin State Journal

ANDY DONATO
Courtesy Toronto Sun

PAUL CONRAD
Courtesy Los Angeles Times Syndicate

MIKE SMITH
Courtesy Las Vegas Sun

MIKE LUCKOVICH
Courtesy Atlanta Constitution

ALAN VITELLO
Courtesy Vitello's View

JEFF MACNELLY
Courtesy Chicago Tribune

BRIAN KELLEY
Courtesy The Signal-Santa Clarita
(Calif.)

MARK PETT
Courtesy Deseret News (Utah)

St. Bill
and the
Dragon

DEFICIT

I HAVEN'T THE HEART TO TELL HIM IT'S JUST ASLEEP

NEIL GRAHAME
Courtesy Spencer Newspapers

ED GAMBLE
Courtesy Florida Times-Union

EDGAR SOLLER
Courtesy California Examiner

ANN CLEAVES
Courtesy The Palisadian-Post (Calif.)

STEVE MCBRIDE
Courtesy Independence Daily Reporter

ROB ROGERS
Courtesy Pittsburgh Post-Gazette

DARYL CAGLE
Courtesy Midweek (Hawaii)

BILL WHITEHEAD
Courtesy Kansas City Business
Journal

JOE MAJESKI
Courtesy Wilkes-Barre Times
Leader

BRIAN FAIRRINGTON
Courtesy Tribune Newspapers
of Arizona

JOE HELLER
Courtesy Green Bay Press-Gazette

PETER DUNLAP-SHOHL
Courtesy Anchorage Daily News

BOB RICH
Courtesy Connecticut Post

JOHN SPENCER
Courtesy Philadelphia Business
Journal

ANNETTE BALESTERI
Courtesy Antioch Ledger-Dispatch (Calif.)

Gradually in the heart of Wall Street Mount Greenspan began to rumble sending bulls and first-time investors running for 401k exit ramps...

DOUG MACGREGOR
Courtesy News Press at Fort Myers

MICKEY SIPORIN
Courtesy Newark Star-Ledger

ARTHUR HENRIKSON
Courtesy Des Plaines Daily Herald (Ill.)

JEFF STAHLER
Courtesy Cincinnati Post

STEVE YORK
Courtesy Kankakee Daily Journal

DREW SHENEMAN
Courtesy Newark Star-Ledger

Competitive Marketplace (Microsoft Version 3.0)

STEVEN LAIT
Courtesy Oakland Tribune

DRAPER HILL
Courtesy Detroit News

ETTA HULME
Courtesy Fort Worth Star-Telegram

"I ASKED HER WHAT'S IN THE PACKAGE. SHE SAID 'IT'S THE ECONOMY, STUPID!'"

EUGENE PAYNE
Courtesy Charlotte Observer

DICK LOCHER
Courtesy Chicago Tribune

TOM BECK
Courtesy Freeport Journal-Standard (Ill.)

MERGER–MANIA, UNABATED...

STEVE GREENBERG
Courtesy Seattle Post-Intelligencer

JOE HELLER
Courtesy Green Bay Press-Gazette

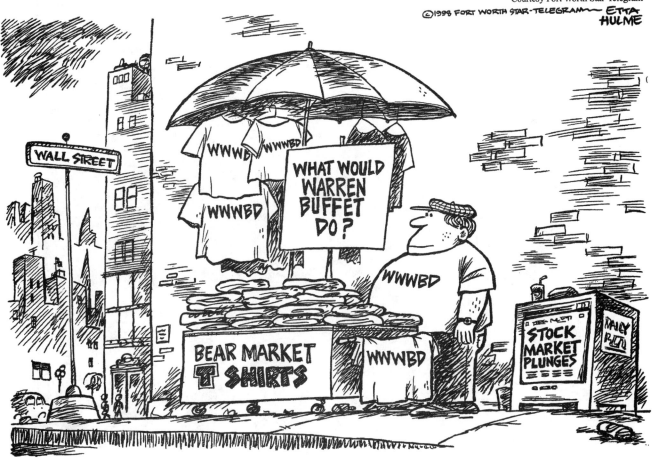

ETTA HULME
Courtesy Fort Worth Star-Telegram
©1998 FORT WORTH STAR-TELEGRAM

TIM HARTMAN
Courtesy North Hills News Record (Pa.)

SCOTT NICKEL
Courtesy Antelope Valley Press

KEN DAVIS
Courtesy Cedartown Standard (Ga.)

Education

Parents and teachers across the country were at a loss in 1998 as to what was causing so much violence in America's schools. More and more youngsters were bringing guns to school. Many states began appointing "school resource officers" trained to identify and counsel troubled youngsters. The programs already have been shown to be helpful.

Two students, aged 13 and 11 and armed with rifles and handguns, killed four of their classmates and an English teacher at a school in Jonesboro, Arkansas, in April. A month later, in Springfield, Oregon, a 15-year-old allegedly fired more than 50 rounds at 400 students in the school cafeteria. Two were killed and 23 were wounded. A search of the shooter's home turned up the bodies of his parents. The incident marked the sixth time in eight months that a U.S. public school was the scene of a fatal shooting.

But while violence in schools was making news, many parents, politicians, and teachers were striving to lift standards and better prepare students for college. President Clinton announced a $400 million plan to spur academic achievement. Educational requirements for good jobs are rising, and parents are insisting that teaching be improved and students get serious about the basics.

DENNIS DRAUGHON
Courtesy Scranton Times

PAUL DUGINSKI
Courtesy Los Angeles Times

VIC HARVILLE
Courtesy Arkansas Democrat-Gazette

MARGULIES
©1998 THE RECORD
www.bergen.com/margulies
JIMMY MARGULIES
Courtesy Hackensack Record

MARK GIAIMO
Courtesy Naples Daily News

E-MAIL: mdgiaimo@naplesnews.com

GUY BADEAUX
Courtesy Le Droit (Ottawa)

DAN O'BRIEN
Courtesy The Business Journal

MICHAEL RAMIREZ
Courtesy Los Angeles Times

WAYNE STROOT
Courtesy Hastings Tribune (Neb.)

STACY CURTIS
Courtesy The Times (Ind.)

STEVE LINDSTROM
Courtesy Duluth News Tribune

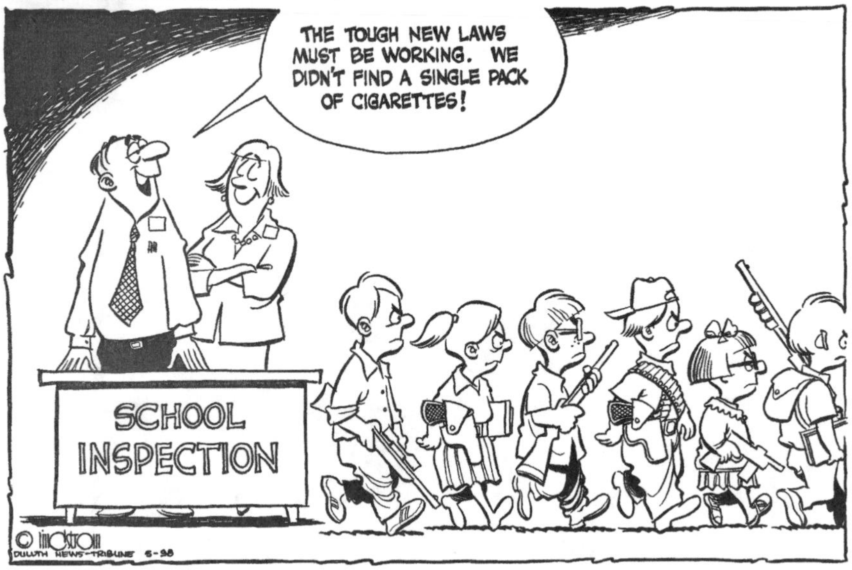
THE TOUGH NEW LAWS MUST BE WORKING. WE DIDN'T FIND A SINGLE PACK OF CIGARETTES!
SCHOOL INSPECTION
© lindstrom DULUTH NEWS-TRIBUNE 5-98

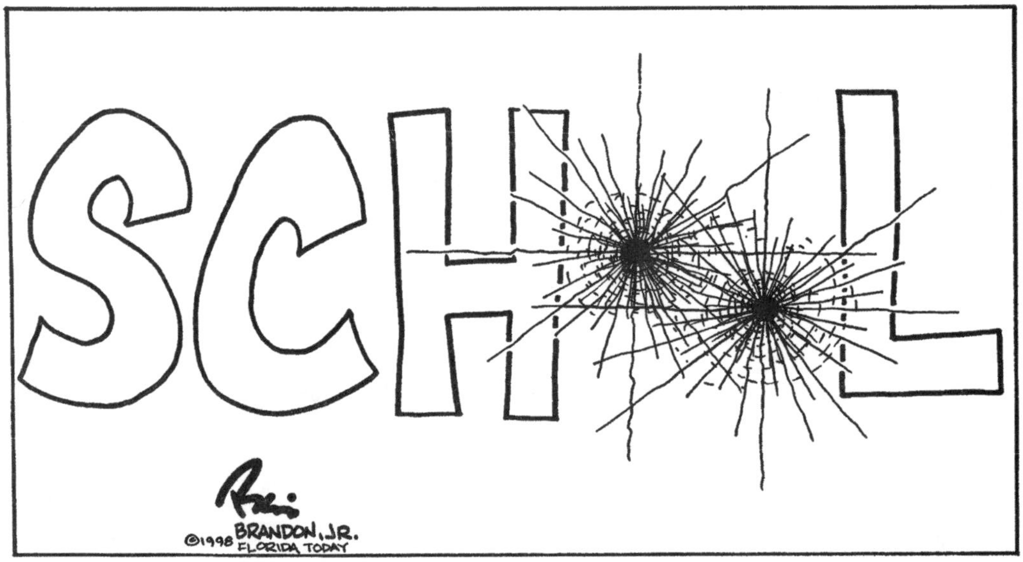
SCH L
©1998 BRANDON, JR. FLORIDA TODAY

BRUMSIC BRANDON, JR.
Courtesy Florida Today

JEFF PARKER
Courtesy Florida Today

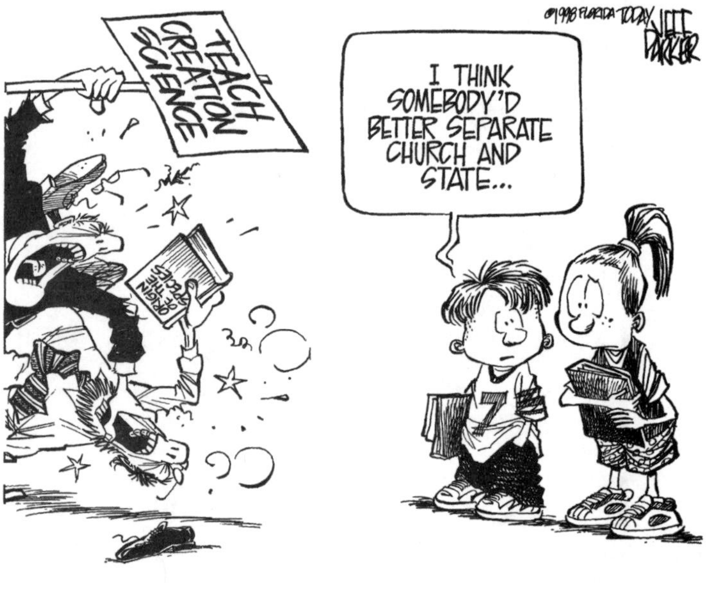
©1998 FLORIDA TODAY JEFF PARKER
TEACH CREATION SCIENCE
I THINK SOMEBODY'D BETTER SEPARATE CHURCH AND STATE...

RICHARD WALLMEYER
Courtesy Long Beach Press-
Telegram

BRUCE BEATTIE
Courtesy Daytona Beach News-Journal

LARRY WRIGHT
Courtesy Detroit News

PAUL FELL
Courtesy Lincoln Journal Star

Crime

Violent crime hit a 30-year low in 1997, according to a Justice Department report released in late December. And the trend is expected to continue. Young Americans, however, are killing each other at a relatively high rate, and hate crimes seem to be on the increase. A gay University of Wyoming student, Matthew Shepard, died after he was severely beaten and tied to a fence post. Dr. Barnett Slepian, a Buffalo, New York, doctor who performed abortions, was murdered by an unknown assailant. And in Washington, D. C., a gunman walked into the nation's capitol and shot two guards to death.

Theodore Kaczynski pleaded guilty to being the notorious Unibomber, in exchange for a sentence of life in prison with no possibility of parole. He was sent to a high-security federal prison in Colorado. Terry Nichols escaped the death penalty for his part in the Oklahoma Federal Building bombing. Pickaxe murderess Karla Faye Tucker became the first woman to be executed in Texas since the Civil War, despite appeals from conservatives such as the Reverend Jerry Falwell, who said she had become a born-again Christian.

James Earl Ray died during the year. Many people still believe he was the fall guy in a conspiracy to kill Dr. Martin Luther King. Dr. Jack Kevorkian was indicted for murder following a live telecast of an assisted suicide in which the noted Dr. Death administered a lethal injection to a patient.

PATRICK RICE
Courtesy Jupiter Courier

JAMES MCCLOSKEY
Courtesy Staunton Daily News Leader

MARSHALL RAMSEY
Courtesy Jackson Clarion-Ledger
(Miss.)

DOMINO EFFECT

PAUL FELL
Courtesy Lincoln Journal Star

MIKE THOMPSON
Courtesy Copley News Service

JOHN KOVALIC
Courtesy Wisconsin State Journal

BOB GORRELL
Courtesy Creators Syndicate

MARK HILL
Courtesy Boulder Daily Camera

CHAN LOWE
Courtesy Fort Lauderdale News /
Sun Sentinel

DON LANDGREN, JR.
Courtesy The Landmark (Mass.)

JOHN SHERFFIUS
Courtesy St. Louis Post-Dispatch

BRIAN FAIRRINGTON
Courtesy Tribune Newspapers
of Arizona

SIGNE WILKINSON
Courtesy Philadelphia Daily News

JIM BORGMAN
Courtesy Cincinnati Enquirer

ROGER HARVELL
Courtesy Greenville News (S.C.)

GROPED BY BILL CLINTON

DAVID REDDICK
Courtesy Anderson Herald Bulletin (Ind.)

HANK MCCLURE
Courtesy Lawton Constitution (Okla.)

JAMES CASCIARI
Courtesy Vero Beach Press Journal

SVEN VAN ASSCHE
Courtesy Darien Times

JERRY BUCKLEY
Courtesy Express Newspapers

VIC CANTONE
Courtesy Brooklyn Paper Publications

ANNETTE BALESTERI
Courtesy Antioch Ledger-Dispatch
(Calif.)

The Environment

The El Nino weather phenomenon, an upswelling of warm air over the Pacific Ocean, brought bad weather to some areas and great weather to others during the year. Heavy rains deluged California and the East Coast, causing massive mudslides and flooding. Tornadoes killed 39 in Florida. A heat wave that baked the Midwest was blamed for dozens of deaths. In Texas, temperatures remained above 100 degrees for more than two weeks.

Hurricane Georges plowed over 17 Caribbean islands, killing more than 400 people and destroying tourism in much of the area. A month later, Hurricane Mitch, the fourth strongest Atlantic storm on record, struck Central America. It killed an estimated 10,000 in Honduras, Nicaragua, and El Salvador and left a million homeless in Honduras alone. The year's hurricane season was the deadliest in more than two centuries.

Studies during the year gave some credence to the theory of global warming. U.S. scientists reported that a detailed study of yearly temperatures showed the 20th century to be the warmest since 1400. British scientists believe the record probably goes back a full millenium. Continuing polar melt caused 75 square miles of an ice shelf called Larson B along the Antarctic Peninsula to crumble and disperse into the sea. The Larson complex has been stable for centuries, but now seems to be breaking apart.

DAVE GRANLUND
Courtesy Middlesex News

MALCOLM MAYES
Courtesy Edmonton Journal (Alberta)

GUY BADEAUX
Courtesy Le Droit (Ottawa)

KYOTO SUMMIT

DOUGLAS REGALIA
Courtesy Contra Costa Times

PAUL CONRAD
Courtesy Los Angeles Times Syndicate

ROADKILL

DENNY PRITCHARD
Courtesy Ottawa Citizen

DAVE GRANLUND
Courtesy Metrowest Daily News

DOUGLAS REGALIA
Courtesy Contra Costa Times

JAMES CASCIARI
Courtesy Vero Beach Press Journal

Health

Congress and health agencies across the U.S., along with the help of the media, took on Big Tobacco in 1998. By mid-year, claims against the tobacco industry exceeded its combined assets. A deal was struck in December whereby 46 states would receive payments totaling $206 billion. The other states were in the process of making their own settlements. Lawyers, of course, were the big winners in these suits.

The drug Viagra, intended to help solve impotency problems among older men, was released, and its use spread like wildfire. Notables such as former Sen. Bob Dole touted its benefits. Late in the year, however, stories concerning Viagra's safety emerged, causing some doctors to wonder if the drug had been released too quickly. Since Viagra was approved by the Food and Drug Administration last March, the agency has confirmed that at least 130 Americans have died after taking the pill. Most of the deaths were from heart attacks.

There continued to be widespread discontent, and in some cases outright hostility, toward health maintenance organizations and the limitations of the health services they provide.

DAVID REDDICK
Courtesy Anderson Herald Bulletin (Ind.)

EUGENE PAYNE
Courtesy Charlotte Observer

PETER DUNLAP-SHOHL
Courtesy Anchorage Daily News

FRIENDLY FIRE

MARK GIAIMO
Courtesy Naples Daily News

ROB ROGERS
Courtesy Pittsburgh Post-Gazette

JOHN SHERFFIUS
Courtesy St. Louis Post-Dispatch

GEORGE DANBY
Courtesy Bangor Daily News

PAUL CONRAD
Courtesy Los Angeles Times Syndicate

PAUL FELL
Courtesy Lincoln Journal Star

RICK KOLLINGER
Courtesy Easton Star Democrat

WAYNE STAYSKAL
Courtesy Tampa Tribune

MICHAEL RAMIREZ
Courtesy Los Angeles Times

ANN TELNAES
Courtesy North American Syndicate

JIMMY MARGULIES
Courtesy Hackensack Record

BRUCE BEATTIE
Courtesy Daytona Beach News-Journal

"Great news! The shareholders have approved your heart bypass!"

ED FISCHER
Courtesy Rochester Post-Bulletin

DENNIS DRAUGHON
Courtesy Scranton Times

MIKE RITTER
Courtesy Tribune Newspapers

CHUCK ASAY
Courtesy Colorado Springs Gazette

Society

For years, it had been rumored. Then, finally, in late 1998 proof allegedly emerged that Thomas Jefferson, the third American president, had taken a slave for a mistress and that she had borne him a son named Eston. It was announced that DNA tests made with the help of descendants pointed to Jefferson as the father of at least one child by Sally Hemmings. The British journal *Nature* conceded later, however, that its report was misleading, and that another member of the Jefferson family could have been the father. The issue was still being debated at year's end.

As the number of states with lotteries continued to grow, studies showed that greater participation by low-income people was the norm. Revenues going to the states from lotteries often are used to improve education, leading critics to declare that the poorer people are simply paying more to operate schools than are the affluent. Liberals continued in the quest to eliminate losers in society. In some schools it emerged in the form of inflated grades and non-competetive sports in which nobody won. Classes are now given on self-esteem and how everyone can be a winner. Societal standards are being lowered more and more. Life does not seem as precious as it once did. Arguments that once were settled peacefully are now often settled with guns. Juvenile violence continues to rise as family values decline in importance to society.

JACK HIGGINS
Courtesy Chicago Sun-Times

JOHN TREVER
Courtesy Albuquerque Journal

EUGENE PAYNE
Courtesy Charlotte Observer

JOHN MARSHALL
Courtesy Binghamton Press
& Sun-Bulletin

MIKE LUCKOVICH
Courtesy Atlanta Constitution

STEVE KELLEY
Courtesy San Diego Union

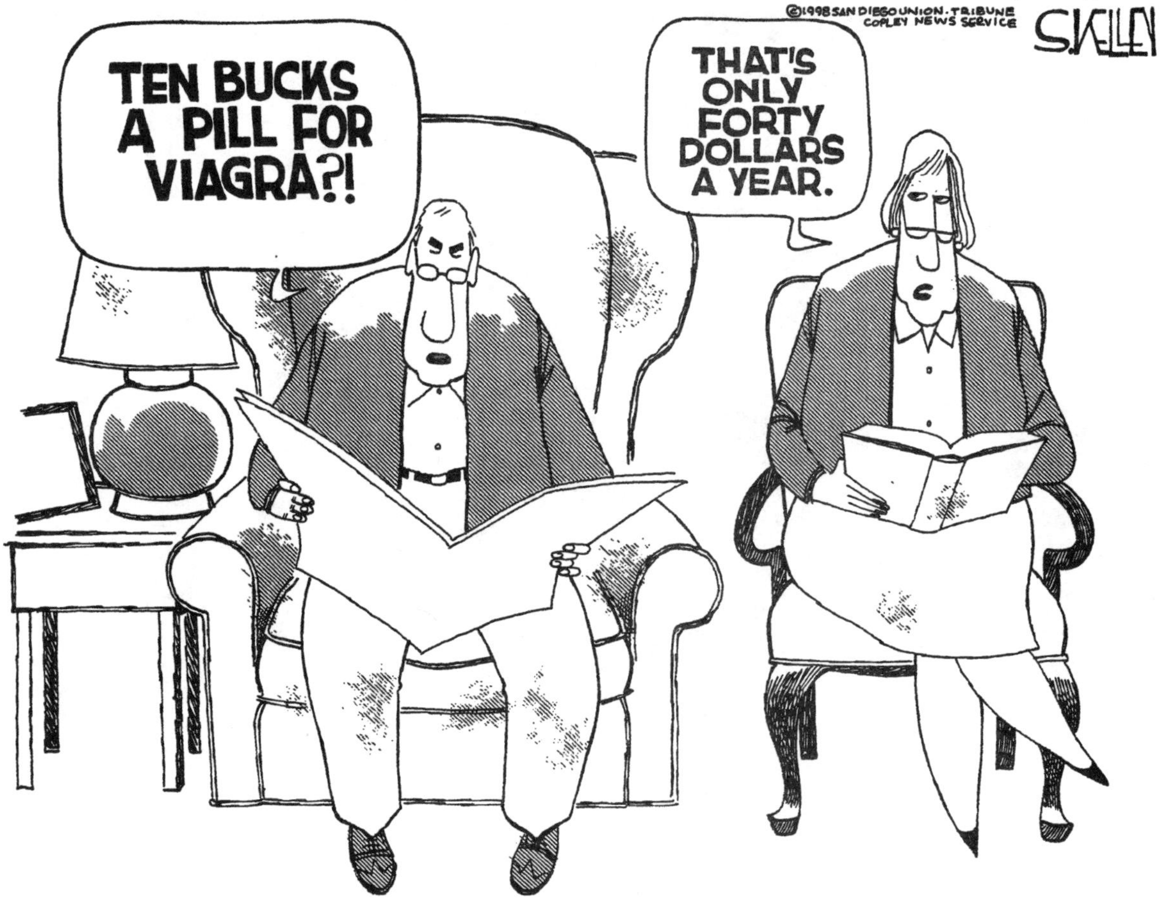
©1998 SAN DIEGO UNION-TRIBUNE COPLEY NEWS SERVICE
S.KELLEY
TEN BUCKS A PILL FOR VIAGRA?!
THAT'S ONLY FORTY DOLLARS A YEAR.

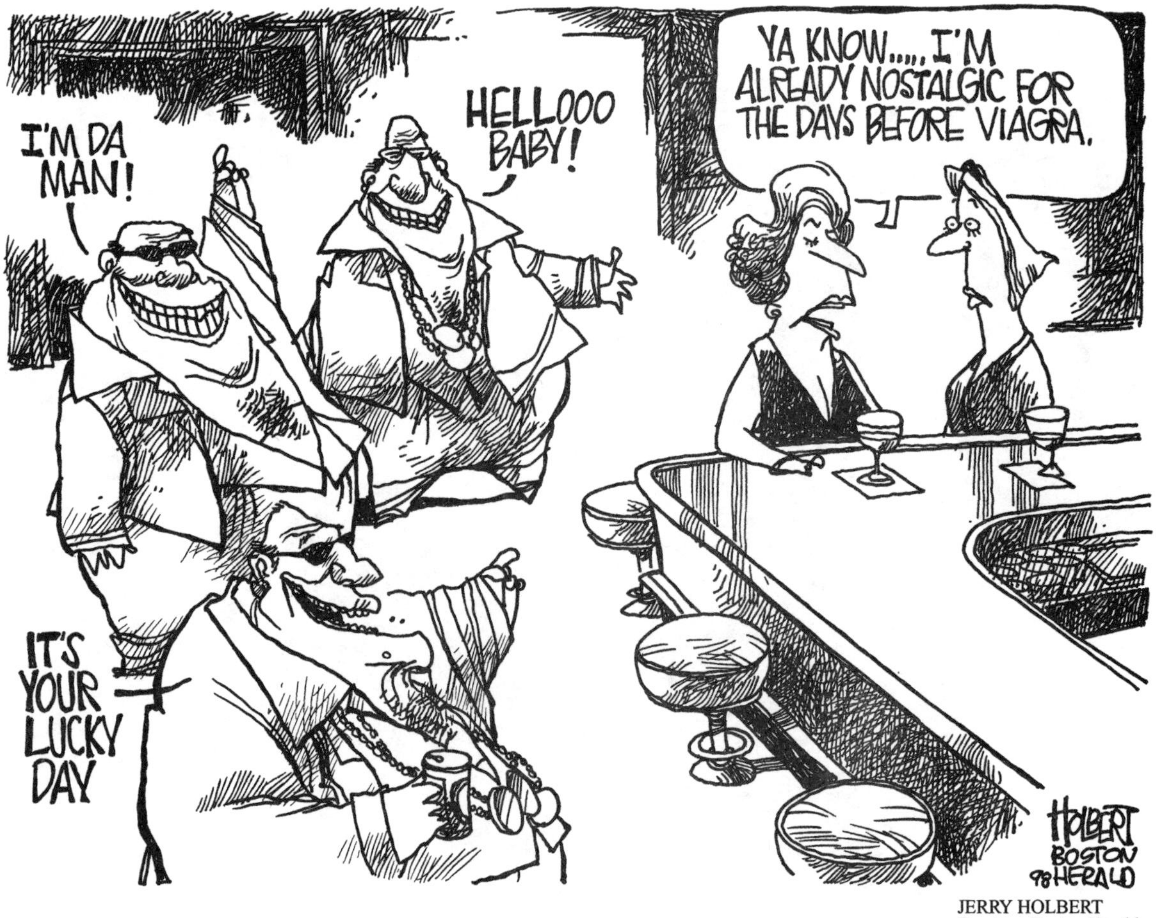
I'M DA MAN!
HELLOOO BABY!
IT'S YOUR LUCKY DAY
YA KNOW..... I'M ALREADY NOSTALGIC FOR THE DAYS BEFORE VIAGRA.
HOLBERT BOSTON 98 HERALD

JERRY HOLBERT
Courtesy Boston Herald

ROY PETERSON
Courtesy Vancouver Sun

DANA SUMMERS
Courtesy Orlando Sentinel

JIM BERTRAM
Courtesy St. Cloud Times (Minn.)

MICHAEL RAMIREZ
Courtesy Los Angeles Times

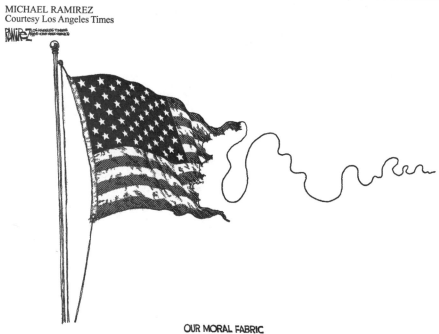

ANN CLEAVES
Courtesy The Palisadian-Post (Calif.)

ED STEIN
Courtesy Rocky Mountain News

STEVE KELLEY
Courtesy San Diego Union

DICK LOCHER
Courtesy Chicago Tribune

WILLIAM L. FLINT
Courtesy Arlington Morning News

ANNETTE BALESTERI
Courtesy Antioch Ledger-Dispatch (Calif.)

EUGENE PAYNE
Courtesy Charlotte Observer

KEVIN KALLAUGHER
Courtesy Baltimore Sun

STEVE BREEN
Courtesy Asbury Park Press (N.J.)

RICK MCKEE
Courtesy Augusta Chronicle

DON LANDGREN, JR.
Courtesy The Landmark (Mass.)

THE SUBTLE EVOLUTION OF THE AMERICAN SOCIAL CONSCIENCE

CHRIS OBRION
Courtesy Fredericksburg Free Lance-Star

BOB ENGLEHART
Courtesy Hartford Courant

VIC HARVILLE
Courtesy Arkansas Democrat Gazette

STEVE BREEN
Courtesy Asbury Park Press (N.J.)

Tomb of the unknowns

MIKE RITTER
Courtesy Tribune Newspapers

RANDY BISH
Courtesy Tribune-Review (Pa.)

The Military

Many books and Hollywood movies have portrayed war as glamorous and exciting. In few films has the blatant horror of war been portrayed accurately. But director Steven Spielberg appears to have achieved just that in his highly acclaimed motion picture "Saving Private Ryan." Spielberg decided to make the movie after concluding that few Americans understand or appreciate the sacrifices made by the nation's fighting men.

In the movie, Sgt. John Miller, played by Tom Hanks, and his men are sent to bring back Private Ryan from harm's way after his three brothers have been killed in action. Then, we see Ryan today, returning to the scene of battle—and wondering if he has led a life that was worth the lives of so many others. The film seems to ask of all Americans: Are we living up to the sacrifices of the World War II generation?

Former Army Sgt. Gene Kinney was sentenced to reduction in rank and reprimanded for obstruction of justice charges following accusations of sexual misconduct. At year's end, many retired military men and others still serving were demanding that Commander-in-Chief Bill Clinton follow the same rules that apply to them.

MIKE KEEFE
Courtesy Denver Post

CHAN LOWE
Courtesy Fort Lauderdale News /
Sun Sentinel

CHESTER COMMODORE
Courtesy Chicago Daily Defender

Another veteran's view of...
Steven Spielberg's
'SAVING PRIVATE RYAN'

"It is good that war grows so horrible, lest we grow too fond of it"
GENERAL ROBERT E LEE

DON MARQUIS
Courtesy Paradise Post (Calif.)

TIM BENSON
Courtesy Argus Leader (S.D.)

JACK JURDEN
Courtesy Wilmington News-Journal

ALAN VITELLO
Courtesy Vitello's View

John Glenn

With a great deal of fanfare, 77-year-old John Glenn returned to space after becoming the first American to orbit the earth 36 years earlier. In the interval, he has spent 24 years representing the state of Ohio in the U.S. Senate. Amid boisterous cheering and parades, his hometown of New Concord celebrated his courage and accomplishments as it had in 1962. Senator Glenn had lobbied NASA to approve the flight in order to study the effects of space on aging. At a time when space flight was being taken for granted and the space program was dwindling in popularity, Glenn's successful flight was a public relations coup for NASA. Russian and American astronauts also joined the Russian-built Zarya control module with the American-made Unity chamber, creating a seven-story tower. The joint venture is intended to establish an international space station.

The U.S. airlines announced that in 1998 no passenger was killed in an accident involving a regularly scheduled U.S. commercial aircraft anywhere in the world. This good news was offset by deaths in smaller, generally propeller-driven commuter planes.

JERRY BARNETT
Courtesy Indianapolis News

171

HANK MCCLURE
Courtesy Lawton Constitution (Okla.)

BRIAN DUFFY
Courtesy Des Moines Register

DANA SUMMERS
Courtesy Orlando Sentinel

ERIC SMITH
Courtesy Annapolis Capital Gazette

JEFF STAHLER
Courtesy Cincinnati Post

LINDA BOILEAU
Courtesy Frankfort State Journal

FRED SEBASTIAN
Courtesy Ottawa Citizen

JOE RANK
Courtesy Rockford Register-Star

SENATOR GLENN REDEFINES THE TERM 'SPACEWALKER'

S. C. RAWLS
Courtesy NEA

DALE STEPHANOS
Courtesy Boston Herald

GARY MCCOY
Courtesy Suburban Journals (Ill.)

REX BABIN
Courtesy Albany Times Union (N.Y.)

Sports

With all the troubling news from the White House scandal and Saddam Hussein's muscle flexing, Americans found a welcome diversion in the homerun record chase between Mark McGwire and Sammy Sosa. It seemed that the whole world was tuned in. Both athletes seemed to possess admirable traits that endeared them even to people who were not sports fans. Both eclipsed Roger Maris' record of 61 homers, McGwire hitting an unbelievable 70 to Sosa's 66. Baltimore Orioles infielder Cal Ripken ended his streak of consecutive games played at 2,632, and the New York Yankees defeated the San Diego Padres in the World Series.

The beginning of the National Basketball Association season was delayed indefinitely when owners and players were unable to settle their differences. The biggest stumbling block appeared to be the union's insistence on reserving 57 percent of team revenues for salaries. The owners conceded on some points, and the players' union offered caps on the salaries of the highest paid players. At year's end, both sides were working hard to salvage the season.

The Nevada State Boxing Commission voted late in the year to reinstate Mike Tyson's boxing license. It seemed to pave the way for another Tyson title shot down the road.

JOHN SHERFFIUS
Courtesy St. Louis Post-Dispatch

JOE LONG
Courtesy Frankfort Observer-Dispatch

"I think I've discovered the cause of your unusual affliction, Mr. Detwyler...
You're a YANKEE FAN, aren't you?"

JIM BUSH
Courtesy Providence Journal

ARTHUR HENRIKSON
Courtesy Des Plaines Daily Herald (Ill.)

JOE HOFFECKER
Courtesy Cincinnati Business Journal

TEAMMATES

JEFF KOTERBA
Courtesy Omaha World-Herald

STANDING OVATION FROM THE UPPER DECK

JOHN BRANCH
Courtesy San Antonio Express-News

MICHAEL CAVNA
Courtesy San Diego Union-Tribune

DANI AGUILA
Courtesy Filipino Reporter

el Dani's Denizens
GREATEST-EVER NY YANKEES SWEEP PADRES TO WIN 1998 WORLD SERIES!
A HALLOW, NOT HOLLOW. WIN!

CLAY JONES
Courtesy Free Lance-Star (Va.)

THE FREE LANCE-STAR
JONES
RESIGN? WHEN HELL FREEZES OV...
NEWS
RIPKEN SITS!
..er.

JOE HELLER
Courtesy Green Bay Press-Gazette

CLAY JONES
Courtesy Free Lance-Star (Va.)

GARY VARVEL
Courtesy Indianapolis Star

JOE MAJESKI
Courtesy Wilkes-Barre Times
Leader

JIM DYKE
Courtesy News Tribune (Mo.)

MALCOLM MAYES
Courtesy Edmonton Journal (Alberta)

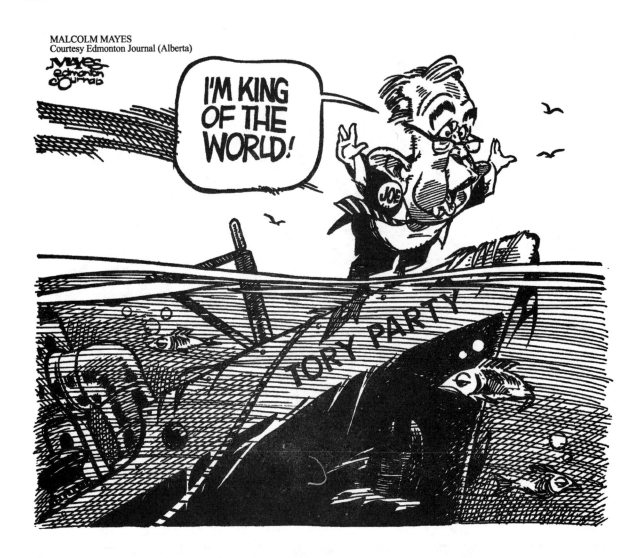

W. A. HOGAN
Courtesy Times-Transcript (New Bruns.)

Canada

Many Canadians were without electric power for several weeks after a devastating ice storm struck the northeastern U.S. and Canada. Jean Charest, leader of the Progressive Conservative Party and a strong federalist, switched to Quebec's Liberal Party in order to challenge Lucien Bouchard, the province's separatist premier. Voters rendered a split decision-of sorts. The pro-independence government was re-elected, winning 75 of the 125 seats to the Quebec Liberal Party's 48. The anti-separatists, however, gained 44 percent of the popular vote to 43 percent for the separatists.

The government's use of pepper spray to control demonstrators during a visit by Indonesia's President Suharto angered thousands of citizens. An investigation resulted in the resignation of Canada's top law enforcement officer.

The Canadian military came in for severe criticism after a story broke regarding the alleged mistreatment of female recruits. Mike Harris and the Ontario government hedged for a time over a settlement with the celebrated Dionne Quints. The Canadian dollar continued to drop during the year. The loonie, so called because of the bird stamped on the face of a dollar coin, was trading at about 65 U.S. cents, down from 72 cents a year ago.

ROY PETERSON
Courtesy Vancouver Sun

GUY BADEAUX
Courtesy Le Droit (Ottawa)

ANDY DONATO
Courtesy Toronto Sun

DENNY PRITCHARD
Courtesy Ottawa Citizen

STEVE NEASE
Courtesy Winnipeg Sun

JAMES GRASDAL
Courtesy Edmonton Journal (Alberta)

ANDY DONATO
Courtesy Toronto Sun

MALCOLM MAYES
Courtesy Edmonton Journal (Alb

STEVE NEASE
Courtesy St. John Telegraph

STEVE NEASE
Courtesy Ottawa Citizer

DENNY PRITCHARD
Courtesy Ottawa Citizen

MALCOLM MAYES
Courtesy Edmonton Journal (Alberta)

189

ROY ROGERS 1911-1998

RANDY BISH
Courtesy Tribune-Review (Pa.)

MARSHALL RAMSEY
Courtesy Jackson Clarion-Ledger
(Miss.)

. . . and Other Issues

Actor Charlton Heston, a staunch political conservative, was elected president of the National Rifle Association, drawing the ire of anti-gun groups across the country. Oprah Winfrey successfully defended herself against a suit by Texas cattlemen who had charged that beef was unfairly linked to the Mad Cow disease on her program.

After hearing from browbeaten taxpayers from throughout the U.S., Congress sent a stern message to the Internal Revenue Service: Clean up your act! The IRS has made motions in the direction of change, but thus far taxpayers have not been impressed. Congress approved a measure allowing Puerto Rico to seek statehood. Even if the Puerto Ricans voted to become the 51st state, it would take years before the action was final.

Two bizarre skiing accidents early in the year claimed the lives of two well-known figures. Michael Kennedy, son of the late Robert F. Kennedy, was killed when he ran into a tree while playing something called football on skis. Five days later, Congressman Sonny Bono died in a similar accident while skiing alone. Other notables who died during the year included Barry Goldwater, Frank Sinatra, Roy Rogers, Gene Autry, Alan Shepard, Shari Lewis, Flip Wilson, and Florence Griffith Joyner.

It was reported late in the year that eight calves had been cloned from an adult cow. Scientists in South Korea claimed to have cloned a human embryo.

JIM BORGMAN
Courtesy Cincinnati Enquirer

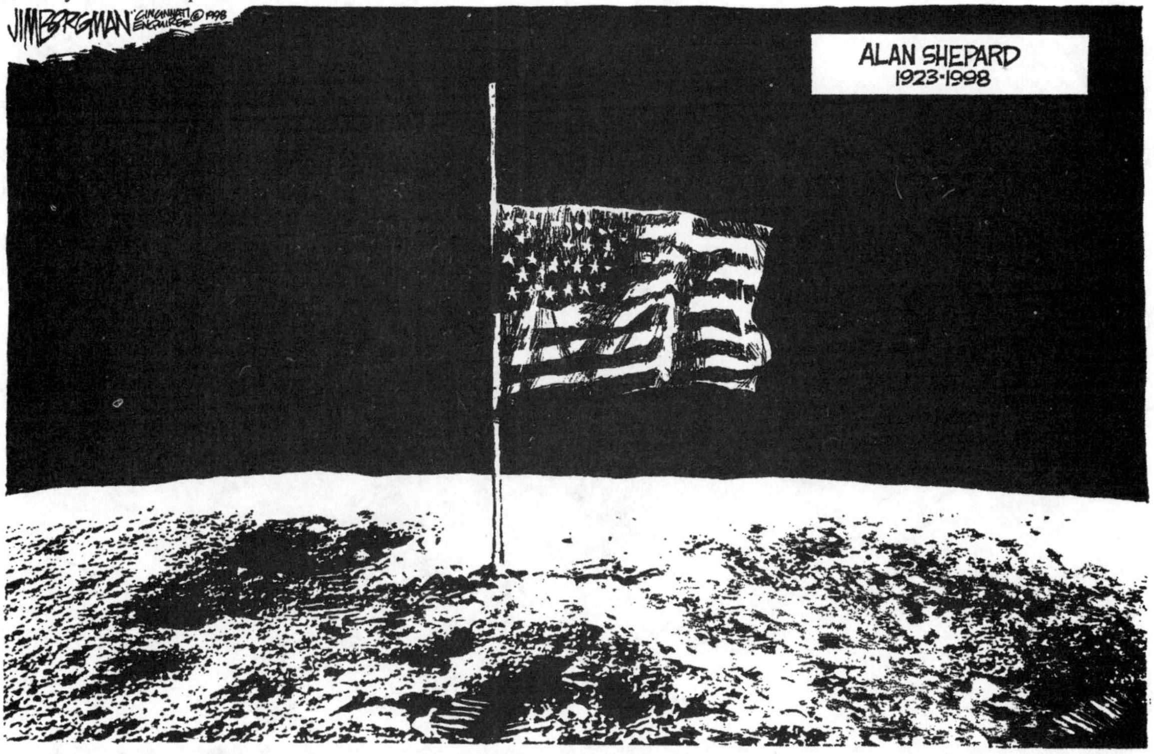
JIMBORGMAN CINCINNATI ENQUIRER ©1998
ALAN SHEPARD
1923-1998

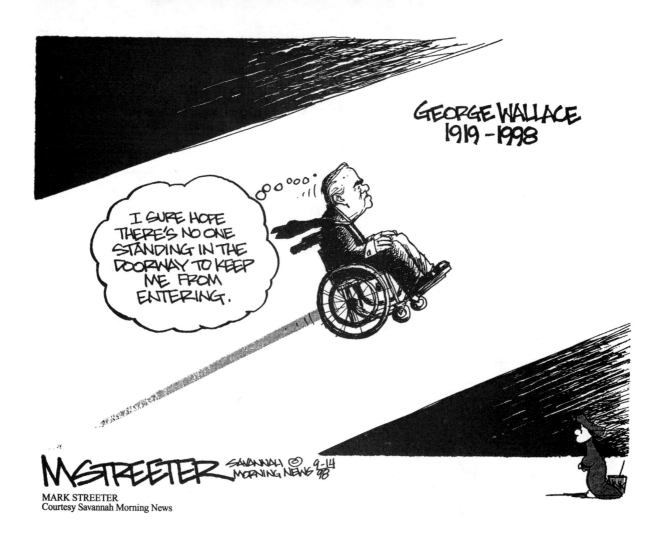

MARK STREETER
Courtesy Savannah Morning News

BOB ENGLEHART
Courtesy Hartford Courant

MICHAEL CAVNA
Courtesy San Diego Union-Tribune

MARSHALL RAMSEY
Courtesy Jackson Clarion-Ledger
(Miss.)

JEFF DANZIGER
Courtesy Los Angeles Times Syndicate

JEFF PARKER
Courtesy Florida Today

DAVE GRANLUND
Courtesy Middlesex News

DAVID JACOBSON
Courtesy White Plains Journal News (N.Y.)

FLOJO -- 1959-1998

JOE MAJESKI
Courtesy Wilkes-Barre Times
Leader

BRUCE QUAST
Courtesy Rockford Register-Star

MARK BREWER
Courtesy The Norwalk Hour (Conn.)

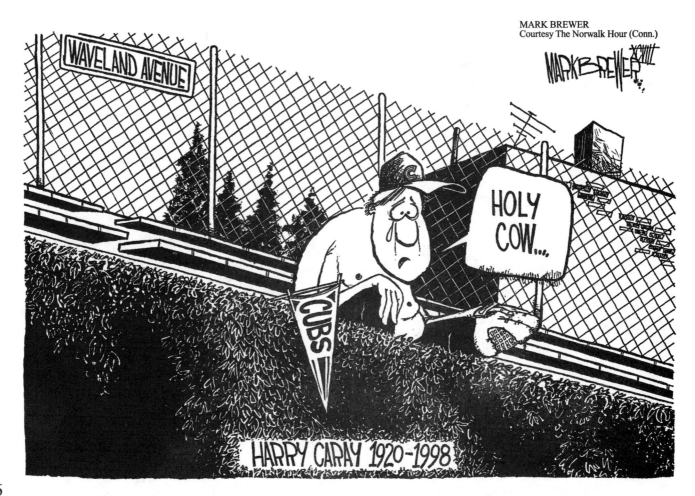

MIKE PETERS
Courtesy Dayton Daily News

FLORENCE • GRIFFITH • JOYNER 1959-1998

KERRY JOHNSON
Courtesy Pittsburgh Tribune-Review

LAZARO FRESQUET
Courtesy El Nuevo Herald (Miami)

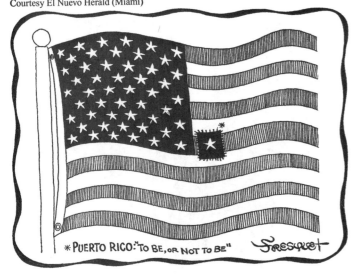

* PUERTO RICO: "TO BE, OR NOT TO BE"

BILL WHITEHEAD
Courtesy Kansas City Business
Journal

ANDREW WAHL
Courtesy Longview Daily
News (Wash.)

WALT HANDELSMAN
Courtesy New Orleans Times-Picayune

BOB ENGLEHART
Courtesy Hartford Courant

JOHN KNUDSEN
Courtesy St. Louis Review

JOHN BRANCH
Courtesy San Antonio Express-News

JACK JURDEN
Courtesy Wilmington News-Journal

RICHARD WALLMEYER
Courtesy Long Beach Press-Telegram

LOU GRANT
Courtesy The Montclarion (Calif.)

THE RED SEA

JEFF KOTERBA
Courtesy Omaha World-Herald

STUART CARLSON
Courtesy Milwaukee Journal Sentinel

Past Award Winners

PULITZER PRIZE

1922—Rollin Kirby, New York World
1923—No award given
1924—J.N. Darling, New York Herald-Tribune
1925—Rollin Kirby, New York World
1926—D.R. Fitzpatrick, St. Louis Post-Dispatch
1927—Nelson Harding, Brooklyn Eagle
1928—Nelson Harding, Brooklyn Eagle
1929—Rollin Kirby, New York World
1930—Charles Macauley, Brooklyn Eagle
1931—Edmund Duffy, Baltimore Sun
1932—John T. McCutcheon, Chicago Tribune
1933—H.M. Talburt, Washington Daily News
1934—Edmund Duffy, Baltimore Sun
1935—Ross A. Lewis, Milwaukee Journal
1936—No award given
1937—C.D. Batchelor, New York Daily News
1938—Vaughn Shoemaker, Chicago Daily News
1939—Charles G. Werner, Daily Oklahoman
1940—Edmund Duffy, Baltimore Sun
1941—Jacob Burck, Chicago Times
1942—Herbert L. Block, NEA
1943—Jay N. Darling, New York Herald-Tribune
1944—Clifford K. Berryman, Washington Star
1945—Bill Mauldin, United Features Syndicate
1946—Bruce Russell, Los Angeles Times
1947—Vaughn Shoemaker, Chicago Daily News
1948—Reuben L. ("Rube") Goldberg, New York Sun
1949—Lute Pease, Newark Evening News
1950—James T. Berryman, Washington Star
1951—Reginald W. Manning, Arizona Republic
1952—Fred L. Packer, New York Mirror
1953—Edward D. Kuekes, Cleveland Plain Dealer
1954—Herbert L. Block, Washington Post
1955—Daniel R. Fitzpatrick, St. Louis Post-Dispatch
1956—Robert York, Louisville Times
1957—Tom Little, Nashville Tennessean
1958—Bruce M. Shanks, Buffalo Evening News
1959—Bill Mauldin, St. Louis Post-Dispatch
1960—No award given
1961—Carey Orr, Chicago Tribune
1962—Edmund S. Valtman, Hartford Times
1963—Frank Miller, Des Moines Register
1964—Paul Conrad, Denver Post
1965—No award given
1966—Don Wright, Miami News
1967—Patrick B. Oliphant, Denver Post
1968—Eugene Gray Payne, Charlotte Observer
1969—John Fischetti, Chicago Daily News
1970—Thomas F. Darcy, Newsday
1971—Paul Conrad, Los Angeles Times
1972—Jeffrey K. MacNelly, Richmond News Leader
1973—No award given
1974—Paul Szep, Boston Globe
1975—Garry Trudeau, Universal Press Syndicate
1976—Tony Auth, Philadelphia Enquirer
1977—Paul Szep, Boston Globe

1978—Jeff MacNelly, Richmond News Leader
1979—Herbert Block, Washington Post
1980—Don Wright, Miami News
1981—Mike Peters, Dayton Daily News
1982—Ben Sargent, Austin American-Statesman
1983—Dick Locher, Chicago Tribune
1984—Paul Conrad, Los Angeles Times
1985—Jeff MacNelly, Chicago Tribune
1986—Jules Feiffer, Universal Press Syndicate
1987—Berke Breathed, Washington Post Writers Group
1988—Doug Marlette, Atlanta Constitution
1989—Jack Higgins, Chicago Sun-Times
1990—Tom Toles, Buffalo News
1991—Jim Borgman, Cincinnati Enquirer
1992—Signe Wilkinson, Philadelphia Daily News
1993—Steve Benson, Arizona Republic
1994—Michael Ramirez, Memphis Commercial Appeal
1995—Mike Luckovich, Atlanta Constitution
1996—Jim Morin, Miami Herald
1997—Walt Handelsman, New Orleans Times-Picayune
1998—Steve Breen, Asbury Park Press

NATIONAL SOCIETY OF PROFESSIONAL JOURNALISTS AWARD (SIGMA DELTA CHI AWARD)

1942—Jacob Burck, Chicago Times
1943—Charles Werner, Chicago Sun
1944—Henry Barrow, Associated Press
1945—Reuben L. Goldberg, New York Sun
1946—Dorman H. Smith, NEA
1947—Bruce Russell, Los Angeles Times
1948—Herbert Block, Washington Post
1949—Herbert Block, Washington Post
1950—Bruce Russell, Los Angeles Times
1951—Herbert Block, Washington Post and
      Bruce Russell, Los Angeles Times
1952—Cecil Jensen, Chicago Daily News
1953—John Fischetti, NEA
1954—Calvin Alley, Memphis Commercial Appeal
1955—John Fischetti, NEA
1956—Herbert Block, Washington Post
1957—Scott Long, Minneapolis Tribune
1958—Clifford H. Baldowski, Atlanta Constitution
1959—Charles G. Brooks, Birmingham News
1960—Dan Dowling, New York Herald-Tribune
1961—Frank Interlandi, Des Moines Register
1962—Paul Conrad, Denver Post
1963—William Mauldin, Chicago Sun-Times
1964—Charles Bissell, Nashville Tennessean
1965—Roy Justus, Minneapolis Star
1966—Patrick Oliphant, Denver Post
1967—Eugene Payne, Charlotte Observer
1968—Paul Conrad, Los Angeles Times

1969—William Mauldin, Chicago Sun-Times
1970—Paul Conrad, Los Angeles Times
1971—Hugh Haynie, Louisville Courier-Journal
1972—William Mauldin, Chicago Sun-Times
1973—Paul Szep, Boston Globe
1974—Mike Peters, Dayton Daily News
1975—Tony Auth, Philadelphia Enquirer
1976—Paul Szep, Boston Globe
1977—Don Wright, Miami News
1978—Jim Borgman, Cincinnati Enquirer
1979—John P.Trever, Albuquerque Journal
1980—Paul Conrad, Los Angeles Times
1981—Paul Conrad, Los Angeles Times
1982—Dick Locher, Chicago Tribune
1983—Rob Lawlor, Philadelphia Daily News
1984—Mike Lane, Baltimore Evening Sun
1985—Doug Marlette, Charlotte Observer
1986—Mike Keefe, Denver Post
1987—Paul Conrad, Los Angeles Times
1988—Jack Higgins, Chicago Sun-Times
1989—Don Wright, Palm Beach Post
1990—Jeff MacNelly, Chicago Tribune
1991—Walt Handelsman, New Orleans Times-Picayune
1992—Robert Ariail, Columbia State
1993—Herbert Block, Washington Post
1994—Jim Borgman, Cincinnati Enquirer
1995—Michael Ramirez, Memphis Commercial Appeal
1996—Paul Conrad, Los Angeles Times
1997—Michael Ramirez, Los Angeles Times

FISCHETTI AWARD

1982—Lee Judge, Kansas City Times
1983—Bill DeOre, Dallas Morning News
1984—Tom Toles, Buffalo News
1985—Scott Willis, Dallas Times-Herald
1986—Doug Marlette, Charlotte Observer
1987—Dick Locher, Chicago Tribune
1988—Arthur Bok, Akron Beacon-Journal
1989—Lambert Der, Greenville News
1990—Jeff Stahler, Cincinnati Post
1991—Mike Keefe, Denver Post
1992—Doug Marlette, New York Newsday
1993—Bill Schorr, Kansas City Star
1994—John Deering, Arkansas Democrat-Gazette
1995—Stuart Carlson, Milwaukee Journal Sentinel
1996—Jimmy Margulies, The Record, New Jersey
1997—Gary Markstein, Milwaukee Journal Sentinel
1998—Jack Higgins, Chicago Sun-Times

NATIONAL NEWSPAPER AWARD/CANADA

1949—Jack Boothe, Toronto Globe and Mail
1950—James G. Reidford, Montreal Star
1951—Len Norris, Vancouver Sun
1952—Robert La Palme, Le Devoir, Montreal
1953—Robert W. Chambers, Halifax Chronicle-Herald
1954—John Collins, Montreal Gazette
1955—Merle R. Tingley, London Free Press
1956—James G. Reidford, Toronto Globe and Mail
1957—James G. Reidford, Toronto Globe and Mail
1958—Raoul Hunter, Le Soleil, Quebec
1959—Duncan Macpherson, Toronto Star
1960—Duncan Macpherson, Toronto Star
1961—Ed McNally, Montreal Star
1962—Duncan Macpherson, Toronto Star
1963—Jan Kamienski, Winnipeg Tribune
1964—Ed McNally, Montreal Star
1965—Duncan Macpherson, Toronto Star
1966—Robert W. Chambers, Halifax Chronicle-Herald
1967—Raoul Hunter, Le Soleil, Quebec
1968—Roy Peterson, Vancouver Sun
1969—Edward Uluschak, Edmonton Journal
1970—Duncan Macpherson, Toronto Daily Star
1971—Yardley Jones, Toronto Daily Star
1972—Duncan Macpherson, Toronto Star
1973—John Collins, Montreal Gazette
1974—Blaine, Hamilton Spectator
1975—Roy Peterson, Vancouver Sun
1976—Andy Donato, Toronto Sun
1977—Terry Mosher, Montreal Gazette
1978—Terry Mosher, Montreal Gazette
1979—Edd Uluschak, Edmonton Journal
1980—Vic Roschkov, Toronto Star
1981—Tom Innes, Calgary Herald
1982—Blaine, Hamilton Spectator
1983—Dale Cummings, Winnipeg Free Press
1984—Roy Peterson, Vancouver Sun
1985—Ed Franklin, Toronto Globe and Mail
1986—Brian Gable, Regina Leader-Post
1987—Raffi Anderian, Ottawa Citizen
1988—Vance Rodewalt, Calgary Herald
1989—Cameron Cardow, Regina Leader-Post
1990—Roy Peterson, Vancouver Sun
1991—Guy Badeaux, Le Droit, Ottawa
1992—Bruce Mackinnon, Halifax Herald
1993—Bruce Mackinnon, Halifax Herald
1994—Roy Peterson, Vancouver Sun
1995—Brian Gable, Toronto Globe and Mail
1996—Roy Peterson, Vancouver Sun
1997—Serge Chapleau, La Presse

Index of Cartoonists

INDEX OF CARTOONISTS

Complete Your CARTOON COLLECTION

Previous editions of this timeless series are available for those wishing to update their collection of the most provocative moments of the past twenty-five years. In the early days the topics were the oil crisis, Richard Nixon's presidency, Watergate, and the Vietnam War. Over time the cartoonists and their subjects have changed right along with the presidential administrations. These days those subjects have been replaced by the Clinton administration, Bosnia, O. J. Simpson, and the environment. But in the end, the wit and wisdom of the editorial cartoonists has prevailed. And on the pages of these op-ed galleries one can find memories and much more from the nation's best cartoonists.

Select from the following supply of past editions

1972 Edition	out of print	1983 Edition	out of print	_____ 1993 Edition	$14.95 pb
1974 Edition	out of print	1984 Edition	out of print	_____ 1994 Edition	$14.95 pb
1975 Edition	out of print	1985 Edition	out of print	_____ 1995 Edition	$14.95 pb
1976 Edition	out of print	1986 Edition	out of print	_____ 1996 Edition	$14.95 pb
1977 Edition	out of print	_____ 1987 Edition	$14.95 pb	_____ 1997 Edition	$14.95 pb
1978 Edition	out of print	_____ 1988 Edition	$14.95 pb	_____ 1998 Edition	$14.95 pb
1979 Edition	out of print	1989 Edition	out of print	_____ Please add me to the list of	
1980 Edition	out of print	_____ 1990 Edition	$14.95 pb	standing orders for future	
1981 Edition	out of print	_____ 1991 Edition	$14.95 pb	editions.	
1982 Edition	out of print	_____ 1992 Edition	$14.95 pb		

Please include $2.75 for 4th Class Postage and handling or $4.75 for UPS Ground Shipment plus $.75 for each additional copy ordered.

Total enclosed: _____

NAME_____

ADDRESS_____

CITY_____STATE_____ZIP_____

Make checks payable to:

PELICAN PUBLISHING COMPANY
P.O. Box 3110, Dept. 6BEC
Gretna, Louisiana 70054-3110

CREDIT CARD ORDERS CALL 1-800-843-1724 or 1-888-5-PELICAN

Jefferson Parish residents add 8¾% tax. All other Louisiana residents add 4% tax.